ENGLISH LESSONS
WITH
MARK PETERSEN

マーク・ピーターセンの
英語レッスン

Mark Petersen

TSURUMI SHOTEN

English Lessons with Mark Petersen

Photo credit:

p.19 © Silvio-stock.adobe.com
p.31 © Bridgman / PPS 通信社
p.43 © Blake Alan- stock.adobe.com
p.73 © yu-photo-stock.adobe.com
p.79 © show999-stock.adobe.com
p.85 © Flor-stock.adobe.com

自習用音声について

本書の自習用音声は以下よりダウンロードできます。予習、復習に
ご利用ください。
（2023 年 4 月 1 日開始予定）

http://www.otowatsurumi.com/0055/

URL はブラウザのアドレスバーに直接入力して下さい。

まえがき

　本書では、一般の日本人、とりわけ日本人の大学生が書く（ときに話す）英語に見られる特徴的なミスや誤解を指摘し、その解決方法を提示してみたが、それだけが目的ではない。英語のネイティヴスピーカーと、共通語として母語ではない英語を使いこなしている人たちの世界観を理解し、感じてほしいと思って作った一冊でもある。そこで、各レッスンを、映画や文学、音楽、歴史、現代社会を特徴づけているトレンドなど、それぞれ異なる文化的テーマを中心にすえた読み物にしてみた。

　私の経験に限っていえば、確かに昔に比べれば現在の大学生の英語の発音と聞き取りはだいぶよくなっているが、同じ大学生が書いた英作文を添削してみると、訂正が必要な箇所は昔と一向に変わっていない。これは、主に中学校・高校で教わったはずの英文法を忘れている、もしくは無視していることが原因のように見える。しかし、「ルール違反」だからまずいとか、与える印象が悪いからよくないとか、そういったことよりはむしろ、誤った書き方によって伝えたい意味が伝わらない、ということこそが問題で、実にもったいなく感じてしまうのだ。

　文の構成と表現の仕方の基礎となる英文法は、英語の論理を理解し、英語を効率よく運用するためのガイドラインとして覚えれば、大いに力になってくれるはずだ。執筆にあたっては、なるべく硬い文法用語を使わないようにしながら、日本語には存在しない時制や冠詞の使い方、正確な前置詞の選択、そして、日本語とは異なる英文の構造などについて、これまでの授業での具体例を交えつつ考えてみた。各章に設けられたエクササイズも解きながら、英語のリアリティを理解し感じていただきたい。

　日本語を母語とする大学生にとって、英語のように根本的にまったく異なる言語を習得することの困難は、長年日本に住んでいるのにいまだに日夜日本語と格闘し続けている「永遠の日本語学習者」である私には痛いほどよく分かる。しかし、この難しさゆえに、伝えたいことが正しく伝わったときの喜びがひときわ大きいことも事実だ。本書を教材にする英語学習者にも同じような喜びを味わっていただければ幸いである。

2022 年　秋

マーク・ピーターセン

Contents

Lesson 1 『陽のあたる場所』で考える冠詞

A Place in the Sun

アメリカ映画 *A Place in the Sun* の邦題『陽のあたる場所』には、不定冠詞の a の意味は表現されていない。しかし、日本語には存在しない冠詞の意味を理解しないと、英文を正確に理解できない場合は頻繁に起こりうる。定冠詞 the も合わせて、冠詞の意味を考える。

Grammatical Points

- 日本語訳で表すことが難しい a と the の意味と用法
- 関係代名詞の限定（制限）用法における冠詞の選択方法

Vocabulary Check

以下の単語の定義を下から選び、その番号を［　　］に入れよう。

appreciation ［　　］	**attain** ［　　］	**conceal** ［　　］
distinction ［　　］	**prominence** ［　　］	**refer to ~ as** ［　　］

1. a difference or contrast between similar things
2. to keep something from sight, to hide
3. to succeed in achieving something
4. to describe or denote someone or something in a certain way
5. the state of being important, especially noticeable, or famous
6. a full understanding of things or situations

A Place in the Sun

The phrase "a place in the sun" is a metaphor commonly used throughout the English-speaking world. It means "a very successful, desirable, or advantageous position." This metaphor attained particular prominence with the success of the award-winning 1951 American film of that title, *A Place in the Sun*, but it was already somewhat well-known for a similar phrase used in the English translation ₅ of an infamous statement made in 1897 by the German Foreign Secretary Bernhard von Bülow. In pushing for the establishment of an expanded German Empire that would rival those of France and Great Britain, von Bülow stated "We wish to throw no one into the shade, but we also demand our own place in the sun." ₁₀

Among the many possible ways to translate "a place in the sun" into natural Japanese, I cannot think of any that would fully reflect the distinctions in meaning to be found here in the use of "a" and "the." Here, "the sun" means "the one and only sun" in our solar system, and "a place" refers to one place among all the other places that are under light from that one sun. There are, however, countless other ₁₅ suns in the Milky Way that have their own solar systems. If we were speaking of "our sun" as one among those other suns, we would refer to it simply as "a sun."

In this regard, I recall once being requested by a Japanese friend to confirm the grammatical accuracy of the following three example sentences for use in an English class: ₂₀

① He saved the boy who everybody thought was dead.
② The woman who we thought was Eri's sister was her mother.

NOTES

1 **metaphor**「比喩」
4 *A Place in the Sun*『陽のあたる場所』1951 年に公開されたアメリカ映画。監督はジョージ・スティーヴンズ、主演はモンゴメリー・クリフト、エリザベス・テイラー。監督賞、脚色賞など、6 つのアカデミー賞を受賞している。
6 **infamous**「悪名高い、評判が悪い」
7 **Bernhard von Bülow**「ベルンハルト・フォン・ビューロー」(1849–1929) ドイツの軍人、外交官、政治家。イタリア大使、外相、ドイツ帝国宰相などを務めた。
7 **push for ~**「~を強く求める、急き立てる」
7 **establishment**「樹立、設立」
14 **solar system**「太陽系」
18 **confirm**「確かめる、確認する」

③ He concealed something in the place which he thought might be safe.

As individual sentences isolated from any specific context, each was certainly grammatically possible. Nevertheless, I suggested the replacement of the "the" in 25 each of them with an "a."

Specifically, with respect to ①"He saved the boy who everybody thought was dead," I explained that the use of "the" would be appropriate only in the following odd and unlikely context: There were some number of boys whom he might have saved, but only one of them was thought by everybody to be dead. He saved that 30 one.

By way of contrast, "He saved a boy who everybody thought was dead" would be appropriate in the following much more likely context: He saved one boy (among all the other boys in the world). It was a boy who everybody had thought was dead. 35

With respect to ②"The woman who we thought was Eri's sister was her mother," in a way similar to that in the previous case of "the boy," the use of "The" here would be appropriate only in the following odd and unlikely context: There were some number of women who might have been her mother, but only one of them was thought by us to be her sister. Her mother was that one. 40

In contrast to this, "A woman who we thought was Eri's sister was her mother" would be appropriate in the following much more likely context: There was a woman (among all the other women in the world). We thought that woman was Eri's sister, but, actually, she was Eri's mother.

Finally, with respect to ③"He concealed something in the place which he thought 45 might be safe," I explained that (once again, similarly) the use of "the" here would be appropriate only in the following somewhat limited context: There were some number of places in which he considered concealing something, but only one of them was thought by him to *possibly* be safe. He chose that one and only place.

Once again, by way of contrast, "He concealed something in a place which he 50

NOTES

25 **nevertheless**「それにもかかわらず、それでも」
25 **replacement of ~ with ...**「~を…と置き換える」
27 **with respect to ~**「~に関しては」
29 **odd**「変わった、奇妙な」
32 **by way of contrast**「対照的に」
37 **previous**「前の」

thought might be safe" would be appropriate in the following much more likely context: There were a number of places which he thought *might* be safe. He concealed something in one of them.

The film *A Place in the Sun* was based on the famous Theodore Dreiser novel *An American Tragedy*, which is about one tragedy among many tragedies 55 that had happened to have occurred in the United States. Its Japanese-language translation is entitled simply *Amerika no higeki* (『アメリカの悲劇』), but, with a basic appreciation of the use of "the" and "a/an," a Japanese learner of English should easily be able to understand why the original title is *An American Tragedy*, not *The American Tragedy*.

60

NOTES ———————————————

54 **Theodore Dreiser** 「セオドア・ドライサー」(1871–1945) 米インディアナ州生まれ。アメリカ自然主義文学の代表的小説家。『アメリカの悲劇』のほかに、*Sister Carrie*（『シスター・キャリー』）などの作品がある。

Exercises

*R**evise the Sentences*

以下の文の冠詞に注意して、正しく書き直してみよう。

1. Once upon a time, there was the young woman who lived alone near a beach.

   ....

   ....

2. Do you like a hotel that you have been staying at for the past week?

   ....

   ....

3. Ukraine is the country in which two languages are widely used. Most native speakers of Ukrainian also speak Russian as a second language.

   ....

   ....

4. The Moon is thought by many scientists to contribute to maintenance of a magnetic field of the earth.

....

....

5. One especially tragic outcome was that the number of people, unable to escape the tsunami, died that day.

....

....

Translate into Japanese

次の名言を和訳してみよう。

1. The only place success comes before work is in the dictionary.

(Vince Lombardi)

....

....

....

2. Tragedy is like strong acid - it dissolves away all but the very gold of truth.

(D. H. Lawrence)

....

....

....

3. A man willing to work, and unable to find work, is perhaps the saddest sight that fortune's inequality exhibits under this sun. (Thomas Carlyle)

....

....

....

....

Translate into English

以下の文を関係代名詞を使って英訳してみよう。

1. 私には秋田に住んでいる弟が（1人）いる。（弟は合計3人）

   ....
   ....
   ....

2. 今のケイトは、20年前の彼女とはまったく別人だ。

   ....
   ....
   ....

3. 火星は太陽系内で2番目に小さい惑星である。いちばん小さいのは水星だ。

   ....
   ....
   ....

Lesson 2 — we の用法について考える

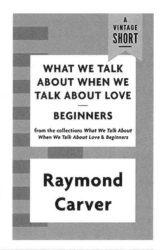

A VINTAGE SHORT

WHAT WE TALK ABOUT WHEN WE TALK ABOUT LOVE
— BEGINNERS

from the collections *What We Talk About When We Talk About Love & Beginners*

Raymond Carver

What We Talk About When We Talk About Love

英語で論を展開するとき、日本の大学生は代名詞 we を多用する傾向がある。しかし、この we が具体的に誰を指すのかが明確でなければ、正確で知的な英文を書き、話すことはできない。村上春樹の著作をめぐるエピソード、そして、大学生が実際に書いた英文などを参考に、we の用法について考える。

Grammatical Points

- 日本人が多用する we は、文中でどのような意味をもつのか？
- 英語で一般論を展開するとき、どのような文体を用いればいいか？
- 「あなた」ではない you の用法を考える

Vocabulary Check

以下の単語の定義を下から選び、その番号を ［　　］ に入れよう。

allusion ［　　］	cliché ［　　］	constrain ［　　］
memoir ［　　］	treacherous ［　　］	weirdness ［　　］

1. to limit or restrict something
2. an expression that indirectly suggests something or someone
3. a phrase or expressed opinion that has been used too often and shows a lack of originality
4. the state or quality of being very strange or bizarre
5. a written record based on personal knowledge, often by a famous person about his or her life and experiences
6. presenting hidden or unpredictable dangers

What We Talk About When We Talk About Love

Raymond Carver is generally considered to have been one of the greatest short-story writers in the history of American literature. In 1981, a particularly influential collection of his short fiction was published under the title *What We Talk About When We Talk About Love*, which was also the title of one of its stories. This story has been translated into Japanese by Murakami Haruki under the title "*Ai* 5 *ni tsuite kataru toki ni wareware no kataru koto*" (『愛について語るときに我々の語ること』). Haruki, the premier Japanese translator of Carver's writing and, of course, a very deep admirer of the author, published a memoir of his own in 2007 entitled *Hashiru koto ni tsuite kataru toki ni boku no kataru koto* (『走ることについて語るときに僕の語ること』). This was later translated into English as *What I Talk About When I* 10 *Talk About Running: A Memoir*.

In 2020, the writer and translator Fiona Bell wrote approvingly of Haruki's use of this title form in a highly entertaining article that was itself (very satirically) entitled "What We Talk About When We Talk About This Title Format." She admiringly reports that Haruki first "asked Tess Gallagher, Carver's widow, for 15 permission to use the title form."

Bell is far less approving, however, when she sarcastically notes, "This title template is most beloved by nonfiction writers, who turned it from a literary allusion into a popular cliché. In 2014 there was Rob Bell's *What We Talk About When We Talk About God*. Sohaila Abdulali published *What We Talk About When* 20 *We Talk About Rape* in 2018 …. Some use this template as either a title or subtitle: *Well: What We Need to Talk About When We Talk About Health* by Sandra Galea

NOTES ————

1 **Raymond Carver**「レイモンド・カーヴァー」(1939–88) 米オレゴン州生まれの小説家、詩人。大学の創作科で教鞭をとりながら、*New Yorker* 誌などで短編を発表。"A Small, Good Thing"（「ささやかだけれど、役にたつこと」）、"Where I'm Calling From"（「ぼくが電話をかけている場所」）などの短編がある。

7 **premier**「最高の、第一位の」

12 **Fiona Bell**「フィオナ・ベル」フロリダ州出身のアメリカの作家、翻訳家、劇作家。ロシア語の作品についての批評、性暴力についての記事を New Yorker 誌などで発表している。

12 **approvingly**「賛成して」

13 **satirically**「皮肉っぽく、風刺をこめて」

17 **sarcastically**「皮肉に、風刺的に」

18 **template**「定型書式、ひな型」

8

in 2019 ...."

Interestingly, Bell states that "the most treacherous word" in this clichéd title format is "we," and the biggest problem is that there is never a clear answer to the question of just who *specifically* is supposed to be included in this group called "we," and who is not. This was not an issue in the case of Carver's story-title since it is clear that its "We" are a group of just four people, two married couples, of whom the story's narrator is one of the husbands.

A problem similar to that pointed out by Bell *can* often be found, however, in the writing in English of Japanese university students. In that writing, using "we" is a very popular way to indicate "people in general" or "all human beings as a group." A typical example of such usage can be seen in this sentence: "We still have much to learn about the origin of the universe."

The problem with their use of "we" is that often, depending on the context, it can refer to so many groups *other* than "people in general." Take, for example, this instance of student writing:

Nature is wonderful. Why do ①we love nature? First, ②we have a tradition of respecting nature in Japan. Also, when ③we get tired from our classes, ④we can enjoy nature to refresh ourselves. For example, from our campus ⑤we can easily go to some natural place such as Mt. Takao.

Here, ①"we" seems to refer to "people in general" and could be replaced by the word "people." This changes suddenly, however, with ②"we," which appears to have a much more limited meaning, i.e., "we Japanese people," and both ③"we" and ④"we" seem to refer to an even narrower group, "we university students." Finally, the meaning of ⑤"we" appears to be constrained still further, to that of "we students at *my* university."

One way to avoid the weirdness of these shifting "we" references would be simply to rewrite the paragraph as:

NOTES

26 **be supposed to ~**「~することになっている」

37 **instance**「実例、事例」

41 **Mt. Takao**「高尾山」東京都八王子市にある山。標高 599 メートル。都心から近いので、近年、多くの登山者を集める。修験道の霊場としての側面ももつ。

48 **reference**「指示する内容、記号の意味」

Nature is wonderful. Why do people love nature? For Japanese people, a 50
long tradition of respecting nature may be part of the answer. For university
students like us, when we get tired from our classes, we can enjoy nature to
refresh ourselves. Students at my university, for example, can easily go from
our campus to Mt. Takao, an area rich in nature.

When "we" is repeated in a series of sentences in a single paragraph, a reader 55
will naturally assume each "we" to be referring to the same group of people in all
of those sentences. When it is not being used in that way, confusion is likely to
result. Student writers should always have clearly in mind who is included in such
a group and who is not included—and be ready to answer the question "Whom do
I mean when I write "we"?

60

Exercises

Revise the Sentences

1. 次の文のアンダーラインが引かれた語を必要に応じて別の単語に置き換えて、自然な英
文にしよう。

Since the 19th century, visitors from around the world have come to Japan to enjoy
cherry-blossom viewing. We often take pictures of ourselves in front of flowering
cherry trees. We also often sit in groups under the trees and enjoy food and drink. We
might naturally think of our famous cherry blossoms as a kind of "national treasure."

....

....

....

....

10

2. 次の文を we を使わないで全体を書き直してみよう。

Italy is a great place to visit on a vacation. First, <u>we</u> can visit many great art museums. Also, <u>we</u> can see a long historical range of architecture, from ancient to contemporary. Finally, <u>we</u> can enjoy delicious regional food in all parts of the country.

....
....
....
....

Translate into Japanese

文中の you の意味に注意しながら、以下の名言を和訳してみよう。

1. You are forgiven for your happiness and your successes only if you generously consent to share them. (Albert Camus)

....
....
....

2. If you're walking down the right path and you're willing to keep walking, eventually you'll make progress. (Barack Obama)

....
....
....

3. Leadership is solving problems. The day soldiers stop bringing you their problems is the day you have stopped leading them. They have either lost confidence that you can help or concluded you do not care. Either case is a failure of leadership. (Colin Powell)

....
....
....
....
....

Translate into English

以下の文を英訳してみよう。

1.「一週間に何時間英語の勉強をしますか？」
　「最低 30 時間でしょうか。そのくらい自分でやらないとものにはなりませんよ」

....
....
....

2. ここ数年、「我々日本人は〜」という表現をよく耳にするようになったと感じるのは私だけだろうか？

....
....
....

3. 昨日の国会で首相は、「いまこそ我々は、これまで培ってきた英知を結集して、地球温暖化に立ち向かわなければならない」と演説した。

....
....
....

Lesson 3 「の」をどう英語に置き換えるか？

Matasaburo the Wind Imp

宮沢賢治の不朽の名作「風の又三郎」。この短編のタイトルは、どんな英語に訳されるだろうか？　問題になるのは、日本語の助詞「の」であるが、単純に英語の前置詞 of をあてることはできるのだろうか？　普段あまり意識することなく使っている「の」と of の用法を通じて、英語と日本語の違いを考えてみよう。

Grammatical Points

- 日本語の助詞「の」は、英語ではどのように訳されるか？
- 「A の B」は、B of A か、それとも A's B で表すべきか？

Vocabulary Check

以下の単語の定義を下から選び、その番号を［　　］に入れよう。

ambiguity［　　］	**appropriate**［　　］	**composition**［　　］
imply［　　］	**literal**［　　］	**posthumously**［　　］

1. suitable or proper for a particular situation or purpose
2. to suggest the existence of something
3. occurring after the death of the person concerned
4. the state of having more than one possible meaning or interpretation
5. an originally created work of music or writing
6. representing the exact wording of an original expression or text

Matasaburo the Wind Imp

Miyazawa Kenji (1896–1933), the great poet and author of children's literature, was, it is sad to say, not at all well-known to the general Japanese public during his short lifetime. It was not until long after his death that he became especially famous and widely admired all across the country.

One of his most valued short stories, "*Kaze no Matasaburō*" (「風の又三郎」), was 5 published posthumously, in 1934. The best translation of this story into English was done by a British man, John Bester, and it did not appear until 1992. One of the first major problems Bester faced was how to translate the title into something that would seem both natural-sounding and attractive in English. The name Matasaburō, of course, could simply be rendered as is, though it is conventional 10 to avoid the use of a macron, as with "ō," in publications that are targeted at a mass market. That is to say, "Matasaburo," rather than "Matasaburō," would be the standard choice. Also, "*Kaze*" (「風」) would present no particular problem either—it could obviously be rendered simply as "Wind." The difficulty was how to express the relationship between "Matasaburo" and "Wind" that was 15 presumably implied by the Japanese-language particle "*no*" (「の」).

In a majority of cases, relationships expressed in Japanese as [A *no* B] can either be expressed in English as [A's B] or [B of A], but there are also a significant number of situations in which only one or the other would be appropriate for use. Even further, there are some situations in which neither would 20 seem to be appropriate. That is the case with "*Kaze no Matasaburō*." A title like "Wind's Matasaburo" would seem to be referring to a person named Matasaburo who was somehow owned by the wind, as a personal possession. In contrast

NOTES
―――――――――――――――

1 **Miyazawa Kenji** 「宮沢賢治」詩人、童話作家、農業研究者。岩手県花巻生まれ。農業指導に従事するかたわら創作活動を続ける。生前に刊行された著書は 2 冊のみだった。「雨ニモマケズ」などの詩、「銀河鉄道の夜」、「グスコーブドリの伝記」などの童話がある。

7 **John Bester** 「ジョン・ベスター」(1927-2010) 日本文学翻訳家。イングランド生まれ。井伏鱒二『黒い雨』、大江健三郎『万延元年のフットボール』など、多数の翻訳がある。

10 **be rendered as is** 「そのままにする」

10 **conventional** 「一般的な、慣習の」

11 **macron** 「母音の上に付ける長音記号」

16 **presumably** 「おそらく、推定するに」

19 **significant** 「かなりの」

to this, "Matasaburo of Wind" would seem to be referring to a person named Matasaburo who was somehow composed of wind, as in, for example, "juice of apples."

The greatest problem faced by Bester would seem to have been that, in the case of "*Kaze no Matasaburō*," no particular relationship between "Matasaburo" and "Wind" was "presumably implied." The possible meaning of the expression is entirely open-ended and left up to the imagination of the reader, and we may assume that Bester, confronted by the impossibility of creating a similarly natural-feeling ambiguity in English, probably decided simply to avoid the issue by making no attempt at a "literal" translation. In the end, he settled on this as a title: "Matasaburo the Wind Imp." In terms of the actual story, the vocabulary choice of "imp" was excellent in its connotation of both childishness and mischievousness. Other translators and commentators have used the term "sprite," which, while it does connote a childlike smallness, does not suggest any particular mischievousness.

One classic example of the "open-ended" possibilities offered by use of the Japanese-language particle "*no*" is *Pari no Amerikajin* (『パリ「の」アメリカ人』), the title in Japanese of George Gershwin's famous jazz-influenced orchestral composition (and also the title of the popular 1951 film in which Gershwin's music was used). The original title in English is *An American in Paris*, which contains much more specific information. It clearly shows that the subject in question is one individual American and that this one American's relationship with Paris is just that he or she happens to be in Paris. By way of contrast, *An American of Paris* would suggest something like "an American whose roots happened to

NOTES

25 **be composed of ~**「〜からできている、〜から成る」
30 **open-ended**「制限のない、再考の余地がある」
30 **left up to →** leave ~ up to …「〜を…にまかせる［委ねる］」
33 **settle on ~**「(〜という選択肢に) 落ち着く、決定する」
34 **imp**「小鬼」
35 **connotation**「言外の意味、含意」
36 **mischievousness**「いたずら好きであること」
36 **sprite**「妖精、小妖精」
37 **connote**「本来以外のものを意味［暗示］する」
41 **George Gershwin**「ジョージ・ガーシュイン」(1898–1937) ニューヨーク生まれの21世紀初期アメリカを代表する作曲家。"I Got Rhythm"(「アイ・ガット・リズム」) や "Summer-time"(「サマータイム」) などのポピュラー音楽以外にも、ジャズに影響を受けた *Rhapsody in Blue*(『ラプソディー・イン・ブルー』) などのクラシック作品も作曲している。

have been in Paris," while *Paris's American* would suggest something like "the one and only American who lives in Paris," an extremely unlikely possibility.

As noted before, though, there are in fact situations in which [A *no* B] can either be expressed in English as [A's B] or [B of A]. One such situation would be, for example, "a poet's skill with words." This could also be perfectly naturally expressed as "the skill of a poet with words." And there are as well, as has also been noted before, situations in which only one or the other would be used. The choice here is generally determined by context. The most important contextual consideration in such cases is usually conciseness of expression, and there are very many contexts in which the use of [A's B] will result in the more concise phrasing. A typical example of this would be something like "last week's typhoon," which expresses in three words what would require five words if "of" were used, as in "the typhoon of last week." 50 55 60

NOTES ──────────────

55 **determine**「決定する」

Exercises

Revise the Expressions

下線部を訂正してより自然な英文に書き換えよう。

1. My daughter never wants to go to <u>a high school of girls</u>.

   ....

2. My grandfather believes that diligence and a little luck are <u>success's conditions</u>.

   ....

3. <u>The paper of today</u> says that the lawmaker was arrested over suspicion of bribery.

   ....

16

4. I can't find many good works in <u>the first decade of the 21st century's literature.</u>

....
....

5. This is <u>a photo of my mother</u>, and, as you can see, she is a very skilled photographer.

....
....

Translate into Japanese

以下の英文を和訳してみよう。

1. "Do you know the Japanese-language title of *The Miracle Worker*?"
   "No. Why don't you look it up on the Internet?"

....
....
....

2. The cost of a surgical procedure usually depends on the individual hospital's billing policies.

....
....
....

3. She often shops at farmer's markets but normally avoids any sellers of non-organic produce.

....
....
....

Translate into English

以下の文を英訳してみよう。

1. 去年に引き続き、彼はまた「父の日」のプレゼントを買い忘れてしまった。

   ....
   ....
   ....

2. 「春分の日」「海の日」「敬老の日」など、日本には 16 もの国民の祝日がある。

   ....
   ....
   ....

3. 彼女によると、医学の発達によって長生きするアメリカ人がだいぶ増えているのに、老後の「生活の質」が悪くなっている。

   ....
   ....
   ....

Lesson 4 論理的な英語を書くために

The Logic of Descartes

「我思う、ゆえに我あり」の言葉で知られるフランスの哲学者ルネ・デカルト。『方法序説』などの著作で人間存在の本質にせまった彼の思想は、現在まで影響を与え続けている。この章では、この名言の和訳に現れる「ゆえに」に当たる therefore をとりあげ、論理的な英語を書くための接続詞や副詞の用法を考える。

Grammatical Points

- therefore, accordingly など論理副詞を使いこなす方法
- and という語の意外な用法
- 英文を書く際の「因果関係」の重要性

Vocabulary Check

以下の単語の定義を下から選び、その番号を〔　　〕に入れよう。

consequence 〔　　〕	furious 〔　　〕	inevitable 〔　　〕
statement 〔　　〕	sympathetic 〔　　〕	rupture 〔　　〕

1. a result or effect of a particular action or situation
2. attracting a feeling of fondness or approval from others
3. to burst or break apart suddenly (often a part of the body)
4. certain to happen, impossible to avoid
5. extremely angry
6. something that someone says or writes that gives information or an opinion

The Logic of Descartes

The most famous appearance of the word "therefore" in English must certainly be this one: "I think; therefore, I am." The sentence is, of course, the ordinary translation of the famous statement by the seventeenth-century French scientist, mathematician, and philosopher René Descartes: "*Cogito, ergo sum*" (Latin) / "*Je pense, donc je suis*" (French).   5

The renowned British art historian Kenneth Clark once called Descartes "an extremely sympathetic figure" and described the following delightful scene. "Descartes … started life as a soldier—he wrote a book on fencing—but he soon discovered that all he wanted to do was to think—very, very rare, and most unpopular. Some friends came to call on him at eleven o'clock in the morning and 10 found him in bed. They said: 'What are you doing?' He replied: 'Thinking.' They were furious."

Descartes had been searching for a statement that could not be doubted, that would, in itself, be undoubtedly true. He found it in "I think; therefore, I am," which could be rephrased as "Because I think, I absolutely must exist." Descartes 15 reasoned that if he doubted the statement, he could not doubt that he himself existed—since it was he himself who was the one doing the doubting. This may seem to be so obvious as to be a fairly silly thing to say. Whatever the case may be, however, for learners of the English language, it is important to remember that the absolute nature of Descartes's "cause-and-effect" reasoning is what makes it 20 possible in English to use the logical connective "therefore."

Here is a perfect illustration of the logical connection implied by the use of "therefore": A = B and B = C. Therefore, A = C. That is to say, "Therefore" here

NOTES ────────

4 **René Descartes**「ルネ・デカルト」[rənéi deikɑːrt] (1596–1650) 本文中にもある「我思う、ゆえにわれあり」という言葉で知られるフランスの哲学者。近世哲学の祖と呼ばれている。

4 **"Cogito, ergo sum"**（ラテン語）[kάdʒitòu ɔ́ːrgou sʌ́m]

4 **"Je pense, donc je suis"**（フランス語）[ʒə pãs dɔ̃(k) ʒə sɥi]

6 **Kenneth Clark**「ケネス・クラーク」1903–83) 英国の美術史家。オックスフォード大学教授、貴族院議員などを歴任。レオナルド・ダ・ヴィンチの専門家として知られる。

7 **figure**「人物」

16 **reason**「推論する、論じる」

20 **cause-and-effect**「因果関係の、原因と結果の関係にある」

21 **logical connective**　文中の論理的関係を表す連結語（句）。

expresses an absolutely inevitable conclusion.

Native speakers of English who teach the language at the university level are often surprised by the frequency at which the word "therefore" appears in the student writing that they are supposed to correct. It seems to be, among students, one of the most popular of all logical connectives, and, for whatever reason, it is used by them far more often than those teachers would ever use it in their own writing. Also, and more importantly, it only rarely survives the correction process.

As we have seen, "therefore" indicates an inevitable consequence, as in, for example, "This morning, Naomi Osaka ruptured her left Achilles tendon. Therefore, she will be unable to compete in the tournament this afternoon." Obviously, it would be impossible for her to compete in a tournament with a ruptured Achilles tendon, and, thus, her being unable to compete is an inevitable consequence of that injury.

By way of contrast, here is a typical example from student writing of the word's misuse: "I was not satisfied with my performance on the field. Therefore, I decided to quit the team." Here, deciding to "quit the team" is by no means an inevitable consequence of the dissatisfaction. There could have been any number of other consequences. The second sentence might just as easily have been, for example, "Therefore, I decided to train harder [ask my coach for advice] [try to get more sleep][etc.]." The most obvious and simplest correction of the original writing here would be to change it to "I was not satisfied with my performance on the field, and I decided to quit the team." Here, "and" is being used in the loosely causal sense that is commonly given for it in English-Japanese dictionaries published in Japan as [*kekka no i wo fukunde*] … *sorede, … nanode* (［結果の意を含んで］…それで、…なので).

Actually, the writing in English of Japanese university students would almost always benefit if their word processors autocorrected "…. Therefore, …." to read "…, and …." since they almost always use "therefore" to express a cause-and-effect relationship for which the "effect" is definitely not inevitable. If they were writing the same thing in Japanese, they would certainly not use "*yue ni*" (ゆえに), as in "*Ware omou, yue ni ware ari*" (我思う、ゆえに我あり).

NOTES

26 **frequency**「頻度」
32 **Achilles tendon**「アキレス腱」
39 **by no means**「決して〜ではない」
49 **benefit**「利益を得る」
49 **autocorrect**「自動訂正する」

Columbia Magazine, of New York City's Columbia University, once published an especially interesting article regarding Descartes by the journalist David J. 55 Craig. In it he discussed the claim that the philosopher had "lifted some of his most influential ideas from a Spanish author and Roman Catholic nun named Teresa of Ávila" and that "historians of philosophy have not drawn a link between the two writers for the simple reason that Teresa was a woman." The title of the article was, very enjoyably, "She Thinks, Therefore I Am." 60

NOTES ───────────────────

55 **regarding** ~ 「～に関して」e メールの返信記号 RE: はこの単語の略。
56 **claim** 「主張」
56 **lift** 「盗む」
57 **nun** 「修道女、尼僧」
58 **draw a link between** ~ 「～の間に関係性を見出す」

Exercises

*F*ill in the *B*lanks

最も適切な副詞を下の {   } から選び、以下の英文の（   ）内に挿入して、文を完成させよう（複数の副詞が入る可能性もあります）。

{ Therefore, Accordingly, Consequently }

1. I ate too much. (   ), I have a stomachache.

2. Richard is only 17 years old. (   ), he is not eligible to vote.

3. The teacher has been hospitalized. (   ), today's class has been canceled.

4. It was clearly established that Evers had received more than 50% percent of the votes. (   ), his election to the governorship was officially certified.

5. The results of the initial DNA analysis have not been confirmed by an independent expert. (   ), many people are unsure of their reliability.

Translate into Japanese

以下の名言を和訳してみよう。

1. Our single most important challenge is therefore to help establish a social order in which the freedom of the individual will truly mean the freedom of the individual. (Nelson Mandela)

....
....
....
....

2. Democracy cannot succeed unless those who express their choice are prepared to choose wisely. The real safeguard of democracy, therefore, is education.

(Franklin D. Roosevelt)

....
....
....
....

3. Absolute liberty is absence of restraint; responsibility is restraint; therefore, the ideally free individual is responsible to himself. (Henry Adams)

....
....
....
....

Translate into English

and と therefore を用いて以下の文を英訳してみよう。

1. 直美は宿題をするのを忘れたので、授業中当てられないようにずっと下を向いていた。
   （and を使って）

   ....
   ....
   ....

2. 原子力発電所の運転に少しでも不具合が生じると、悲惨な放射能漏れが発生する可能性
   がある。そのため、入念なメンテナンスが重要だと考えられている。（therefore を使って）

   ....
   ....
   ....

3. ロシア軍はかなりの兵力を失ったので、ウクライナとの国境地域まで退却しなければな
   らなかった。（and を使って）

   ....
   ....
   ....

Lesson **5** 『怒りの葡萄』で学ぶ比較級

As High as the Fence Tops

世界恐慌と、「ダストボウル」という大災害を背景に描かれたスタインベックの小説『怒りの葡萄』。1939 年に書かれたこの作品に描かれる環境破壊、貧困などの問題は、現代世界にも強いメッセージを放ち続ける。アメリカ中部を襲った砂嵐についての英語表現から、日本語に訳すと正確さが失われる比較級の問題について考える。

Grammatical Points

- 論比較級、as 〜 as や no other 〜 as [than] の正確な意味と用法
- 比較級を使った様々な表現

Vocabulary Check

以下の単語の定義を下から選び、その番号を [　　] に入れよう。

crucial [　　]	encounter [　　]	epic [　　]
expedient [　　]	reference to [　　]	relevant [　　]

1. a convenient and practical way of achieving a desired outcome, though one that may possibly be improper or immoral
2. mention of
3. closely connected to or appropriate with regard to something
4. extremely important or necessary, vital
5. a movie, book, poem, or other work that tells a long story about heroic deeds or historical events
6. to meet someone or something unexpectedly

As High as the Fence Tops

🎧
13

Once, when doing some research on the Nobel Prize winning American novelist John Steinbeck, I came across a strange piece of information during a Google search. It was said that his name had been adopted as a character-name in a Japanese manga and anime series entitled *Bungo Stray Dogs*. A further search indicated that one of the series' characters was, indeed, called "*Jon Sutainbekku*" 5 (ジョン・スタインベック), and that his "superpower" was called "*Ikari no budō*" (怒り の葡萄), a reference to the real-life Steinbeck's greatest achievement, his epic novel of realism *The Grapes of Wrath*. Not being fond of the fantasy genre in any form, I was not tempted to read or view *Bungo Stray Dogs* itself, but the reference did cause me to wonder about the extent to which Steinbeck's extraordinary *The* 10 *Grapes of Wrath* was actually known and read in contemporary Japan.

The long novel begins in Oklahoma, a state in the South-Central region of the U.S. Its first chapter is a vivid description of the effects of the Dust Bowl, the terrible ecological disaster of the 1930s which devastated great stretches of prairie land across North America. The issue of the Dust Bowl is especially relevant 15 today because its causes—severe drought and poor agricultural practices—are the same ones that continue, even now, to result in misery, famine, mass migration, and death in many areas of the world.

NOTES

2 **John Steinbeck**「ジョン・スタインベック」(1902–68)　米カリフォルニア州出身の作家。 貧しい農業従事者と社会との関係について多くの小説を執筆した。『怒りの葡萄』のほかに *Of Mice and Men*（『二十日鼠と人間』）、*East of Eden*（『エデンの東』）などの代表作がある。 1962 年、ノーベル文学賞受賞。
3 **adopt**「採用する、借用する」
4 ***Bungo Stray Dogs***『文豪ストレイドッグス』日本をはじめ世界の文豪たちが登場し、闘 うアクションマンガ。朝霧カフカ（原作）、春河 35（作画）。『ヤングエース』(KADO-KAWA) で 2013 年から連載中。
9 **be tempted to ~**「～する気にさせられる」
10 **extraordinary**「非凡な、並外れた」
13 **vivid**「強烈な、鮮やかな」」
14 **devastate**「荒廃させる」
14 **prairie**「大草原、プレーリー」
16 **drought**「干ばつ、日照り」
17 **famine**「飢饉」
17 **mass migration**「集団移住」

14

Below is the third paragraph of Chapter 1, which accurately conveys the feeling of Steinbeck's writing. To understand it, it is important to know that, in rural 20 Oklahoma of the 1930s, roads were still largely unpaved, as they also were in almost all of rural Japan at that time, and that horses and mules were still crucial to the plowing of fields and the pulling of wagons.

> In the roads where the teams moved, where the wheels milled the ground and the hooves of the horses beat the ground, the dirt crust broke and the dust 25 formed. Every moving thing lifted the dust into the air: a walking man lifted a thin layer as high as his waist, and a wagon lifted the dust as high as the fence tops, and an automobile boiled a cloud behind it. The dust was long in settling back again.

For a Japanese learner of the English language, no better education could be 30 provided than by a careful, guided reading of *The Grapes of Wrath* in its entirety. Even the short paragraph above contains two examples of a form in English that is often misunderstood by such learners of the language: "as high as his waist" and "as high as the fence tops." The source of the misunderstanding lies in the fact that the form <as ~ as …> is so often translated into Japanese using the expression 35 "… *to onaji kurai*" (…と同じくらい). This manner of translation is simply an expedient, offering the easiest way to create an expression that feels "natural" in Japanese, even though it may not have exactly the same meaning as that of the original English.

15

Specifically, in "as high as his waist" and "as high as the fence tops," the use of 40 "… *to onaji kurai*" indicates that the "dust" could have reached levels that were either slightly higher or slightly lower than, respectively, those of "his waist" and

---

NOTES

21 **unpaved**「舗装していない、敷石を敷いていない」
22 **mule**「ラバ」
23 **plow**「鍬（くわ）で耕す」
24 **teams**「(荷車などを引く) 二頭以上の馬」
24 **mill**「ひいて粉にする」
25 **hooves**「hoof (ひづめ) の複数形」
25 **dirt crust**「地表」
28 **boil**「(沸騰して) 沸き上がらせる」
31 **entirety**「全体、全部」
42 **respectively**「それぞれ、別々に」

"the fence tops." In fact, however, this is a fundamental inaccuracy. Basically, "as high as his waist" and "as high as the fence tops" mean that the dust could have reached levels that were, respectively, the same as or higher than those of "his waist" and "the fence tops," but not levels that were even slightly lower. 45

This reminds me of a similar misunderstanding I once encountered in grading the results of an English exam. In it, examinees had been asked to write a sentence in English, using the expression "No other ....", that would have the same meaning as the sentence "Mt. Kilimanjaro is the highest mountain in Africa." The 50 correct answer is, of course, "No other mountain in Africa is as high as Mt. Kilimanjaro," but, for some reason, the most common answer given was "No other mountain in Africa is higher than Mt. Kilimanjaro." The misunderstanding here lies in a failure to realize that this answer allows for the possibility that there may be one or more mountains in Africa that are of the same height as Mt. 55 Kilimanjaro (but none that are higher). Since, however, Mt. Kilimanjaro is the highest, no other mountain could possibly be of the same height.

NOTES ————

50 **Mt. Kilimanjaro**「キリマンジャロ山」タンザニア北部にある火山。

Exercises

*F*ill in the *B*lanks

日本語の意味を参考に（　　　）内に適切な英単語を入れて英文を完成させよう。

1. その作家の新作は、前作の2倍の長さだ。

   The author's latest book is (　　　) (　　　) (　　　) (　　　) her last work.

2. ジョージはプロのミュージシャンになろうとしていたわけではない。ましてやロック・スターなどになろうとは思っていなかった。

   George didn't set out to become a professional musician, (　　　) (　　　) a rock star.

3. 大統領による新しい教育政策は、ほぼ完璧と言っていい。改善の余地はほぼない。

   The President's new education policy can be said to be nearly perfect. It could hardly (　　　　) (　　　　　　　).

4. このことは100年前に劣らず現在も真実である。

   This is (　　　) (　　　　　) true today than it was one hundred years ago.

5. 彼ほど腐敗して誇大妄想にとりつかれた男に投票するなど、有権者はうかつだった。

   Voters should have (　　　　) (　　　　　) than to vote for a man so corrupt and megalomaniac as he.

Translate into Japanese

以下の名言を和訳してみよう。

1. Nothing in all the world is more dangerous than sincere ignorance and conscientious stupidity. (Martin Luther King, Jr.)

   ....
   ....
   ....

2. The more you like yourself, the less you are like anyone else, which makes you unique. (Walt Disney)

   ....
   ....
   ....

3. It is better to keep your mouth closed and let people think you are a fool than to open it and remove all doubt. (Mark Twain)

....
....
....

Translate into English

以下の日本語を英訳してみよう。

1. 富士山は日本で一番高い山だ。(no other を用いて)

....
....

2. 1000 語以上で、『怒りの葡萄』についてのエッセイを書け。

....
....

3. 1918 年から数年にわたって世界で流行したスペイン風邪により、世界で 5000 万人以上の人が亡くなったと言われている。(no fewer than を用いて)

....
....
....

Lesson **6** 映画のタイトルから考える現在完了形

You've Got Mail

日本で公開される外国映画は、独自のタイトルが付けられる場合と、英語など元の言語が
カタカナに置き換えられる場合に大きく二分できる。特にカタカナ英語のタイトルに限っ
て言えば、冠詞や複数形が省略されるために、本来のニュアンスが伝わらないことが多い。
普段何気なく見かけるタイトルを考えることで浮き上がってくる、時制の問題も考える。

*G*rammatical *P*oints

- 現在完了形と過去形の違い
- 現在完了形を使いこなす方法
- 省略された映画のタイトルには表れない、正確な英語の意図

*V*ocabulary *C*heck

以下の単語の定義を下から選び、その番号を [　　] に入れよう。

appreciate [　　]	approximate [　　]	distribution [　　]
evocative [　　]	thrive [　　]	unwieldy [　　]

1. to realize the full worth or importance of something
2. the act of transporting or delivering products to a number of people or companies
3. difficult to handle because of its content, shape, or size
4. close to being exact but not completely exact
5. bringing strong images or feelings to mind
6. to grow well, to develop vigorously, to progress successfully

You've Got Mail

In 1998, the filmmaker and writer Nora Ephron followed her surprisingly successful 1993 rom-com (romantic comedy) film *Sleepless in Seattle* with another rom-com hit, *You've Got Mail*, starring the same two actors, Tom Hanks and Meg Ryan. Some people love rom-coms, while others, quite naturally, find many of them to be so saccharine as to be unwatchable, but no matter what one might think 5 of such movies, Ephron's work was in an extremely long and unending tradition. The first rom-com is said to have been the silent film *All for a Girl* (1912), and the genre has continued to thrive into the 2020s, with such typical examples as *Marry Me* (2022).

It is always interesting to see the Japanese-language titles that distribution 10 companies in Japan choose to attach to English-language films like these before their domestic release. Back in 1993, it was perhaps still slightly more common than today to use the approach seen in the case of *Sleepless in Seattle*, which, for Japanese audiences, was entitled *Meguriaetara* (『めぐり逢えたら』). In this approach, there is no attempt to "translate" the title; rather, an entirely new title is assigned, 15 one that is presumably thought to be appropriately "evocative." This style was also adopted for the 1994 drama *The Shawshank Redemption*, which became *Shōshanku no sora ni* (『ショーシャンクの空に』), and even more dramatically for Disney's 2013 computer-animated musical fantasy *Frozen*, which came out as *Ana to yuki no joō* (『アナと雪の女王』).

20

At present, however, it seems to be more common to employ a much easier

---

NOTES

1 **Nora Ephron**「ノーラ・エフロン」(1941–2012) ニューヨーク生まれの映画監督。*Silkwood*（『シルクウッド』1983年公開）、*When Harry Met Sally ...*（『恋人たちの予感』1989年公開）などの脚本も担当していた。

3 **Tom Hanks**「トム・ハンクス」(1956–) カリフォルニア州出身の俳優、映画監督。1993年公開の *Philadelphia*（『フィラデルフィア』）と翌年公開の *Forrest Gump*（『フォレスト・ガンプ／一期一会』）で2年連続アカデミー主演男優賞を受賞している。

3 **Meg Ryan**「メグ・ライアン」(1961–) コネティカット州出身の俳優。*When Harry Met Sally ...*（『恋人たちの予感』）など多くの恋愛コメディの主演を務め、「ロマンティック・コメディの女王」と呼ばれる。

5 **saccharine**「甘ったるい」

12 **domestic**「自国内の」

15 **assign**「割り当てる、与える」

21 **employ**「用いる、利用する」

approach: using *katakana* to simply give an approximate transliteration of the original English. In this way, *Marry Me* became *Marī mī* (『マリー・ミー』). Sometimes, unfortunately, this results in a title whose actual meaning would likely be incomprehensible to almost all ordinary Japanese citizens, as was the case when the 1999 "sports drama" *Any Given Sunday* became *Enī gibun sandē* (『エニイ・ギブン・サンデー』).

For native speakers of English, there is a more troubling element to be found in titles that have been given an "approximate transliteration." It is the deleting of elements from the original that have significance in terms of English meaning. A typical example of this is the change from *The Cider House Rules* (a 1999 drama) to *Saidāhausu rūru* (『サイダーハウス・ルール』), by which the important initial "The" was eliminated, as was the "s" at the end of "Rules" (the "s" clearly expresses the existence of multiple rules). Undoubtedly, the very concise *Saidāhausu rūru* was simply thought to sound better than would a more precise but somewhat unwieldy *Za saidā hausu rūruzu* (『ザ・サイダー・ハウス・ルールズ』), and, in any case, the deletions would be unlikely to have any particular significance for the average Japanese citizen.

One especially striking similar case is that of Ephron's *You've Got Mail*, which became *Yū gatto mēru* (『ユー・ガット・メール』=You Got Mail). For learners of English, it is very important to realize the complete difference in meaning between the two sentences "You got mail" and "You've got [= have got] mail." The sentence "You got mail" simply means that at least once, sometime in the past, you received some email. In contrast to this, the alert message "You've got mail" means that you have received some email which, currently, you have not yet opened. The meaning would not change if the alert message were phrased as "You have mail," or even as "You currently have some unopened mail to look at."

The average Japanese learner of English might well be forgiven for not necessarily appreciating the difference in meaning between these two sentences,

---

NOTES

22 **transliteration** 「音訳、翻字」ある文字の表記を、その発音に基づいて別の文字で表すこと。

25 **as was the case when** ~「~であるときと同様に」

32 **initial** 「初めの」

33 **be eliminated** 「省かれる、除去される」

34 **existence** 「存在」

35 **precise** 「正確な、的確な」

46 **be phrased as** ~「~と表現される」

as, in junior high school English textbooks in Japan, the past tense may often 50
be used in situations which would actually call for the present perfect. Here is
a simple example once found in such a textbook: "'You changed my life, Jane,'
he said." While this sentence notes the occurrence of a "change" in the past, it
says nothing about the present; it is entirely possible that the speaker's life has
since returned to what it had originally been. From the context of the textbook's 55
story, however, it is clear that such is not the case. Actually, the speaker's "life"
currently remains in the same "changed" condition. In order to express that fact,
it is necessary to use the present perfect tense and to write: "'You've [You have]
changed my life, Jane,' he said."

Another previously discovered example of this phenomenon was in the story of 60
a new invention. The inventor says, "But I didn't try it yet." Obviously, the "yet"
means "still, as of now," and in real English the sentence would be "But I haven't
tried it yet."

NOTES ————————————————

53 **occurrence**「発生、出現」

Exercises

Make Corrections

日本語を参考に、次の文の間違いを正そう。

1. 健は過去 20 年間、ビートルズのレコード盤を集めている。

   Ken collects vinyl records by the Beatles for the last twenty years.

   ....

2. 私は今日の午前中にスマートフォンを買ったが、まだ試していない。

   I bought a new smartphone this morning, but I didn't try it yet.

   ....

3. 大谷は、昨日ついに大リーグの新しい球団と契約を結んだ。

Ohtani has finally signed with a new major league team yesterday.

....

4. 大学にいる間、何かボランティアをしましたか？

Have you ever done any volunteer work while you were in university?

....

5. ジョンは東京に引っ越してくる前に、バンクーバーに5年間住んでいた。

John has lived in Vancouver for five years before moving to Tokyo.

....

Translate into Japanese

次の名言を和訳してみよう。

1. Don't part with your illusions. When they are gone, you may still exist, but you have ceased to live. (Mark Twain)

....
....
....

2. Unless you try to do something beyond what you have already mastered, you will never grow. (Ralph Waldo Emerson)

....
....
....

3. What experience and history teach is this—that nations and governments have never learned anything from history, or acted upon any lessons they might have drawn from it. (G. W. F. Hegel)

....
....
....
....

Translate into English

次の文を英訳してみよう。

1. 私がピカソの絵画を見るのは、これが初めてです。

....
....

2. 来年の３月で、ピーターが日本で暮らして 50 年になる。

....
....

3. 2022 年のロシアのウクライナ侵攻以来、世界中で光熱費が急激に上昇している。各国は、エネルギー政策の早急な転換が求められている。

....
....
....

Lesson 7　小さな副詞 "so" がもつ意味と効果的な用法

So Many Worlds,
So Much to Do

> so は、日本語が母語の英語学習者が気軽に使う副詞の一つだが、very の代わりに使うという「誤用」が大きく浸透してしまっている。イギリスの元首相チャーチル、そして同じくイギリスの詩人テニスンが残した名言を読み解きながら、この小さな副詞がもつ意味と効果的な用法を考えてみよう。

Grammatical Points

- so の正しい用法を考える
- so と very を文意に従って使い分ける方法を学ぶ

Vocabulary Check

以下の単語の定義を下から選び、その番号を ［　　］に入れよう。

abbreviation ［　　］	**grieve** ［　　］	**idiomatic** ［　　］
mastery ［　　］	**numerically** ［　　］	**oratory** ［　　］

1. containing expressions that are natural to a native speaker of a language

2. the skill and practice of making formal speeches in public

3. in terms of numbers

4. to feel deep sadness

5. a shortened form of a word or phrase

6. comprehensive knowledge of a particular subject or skill in a particular activity

So Many Worlds, So Much to Do

19

　The 1953 Nobel Prize in Literature was awarded to Winston Churchill "for his mastery of historical and biographical description as well as for brilliant oratory in defending exalted human values." Churchill's most important works of non-fiction writing, his twelve-volume memoir *The Second World War* and his four-volume *A History of the English-Speaking Peoples*, are still widely read, but it is surely his 5 remarkable oratorical skills for which he is best remembered today.

　One of his most inspiring rhetorical flourishes came in a speech to the British House of Commons on August 20, 1940, when he was the nation's wartime Prime Minister. In gratitude for the heroic efforts of the pilots of the Royal Air Force (as well as for those of a number of pilots from allied countries) in defending Britain 10 from attacks by the numerically vastly superior German Luftwaffe during the crucial Battle of Britain, Churchill famously stated "Never in the field of human conflict was so much owed by so many to so few."

　For learners of English, the oft-quoted "so much owed by so many to so few" provides a perfect example of one of the most important uses of "so" as an 15 adverb: indicating "to such a great extent." In Japanese-language translations of Churchill's speech, the most commonly employed adverb seems to be "*kakumo*" (かくも), but "*korehodo*" (これほど) can also be found, and both convey the same sense of "to such a great extent."

NOTES ———————————

1 **Winston Churchill**「ウインストン・チャーチル」(1874–1965) イギリスの政治家。1940–45 年、1951–55 年の 2 度首相を務める。

3 **exalted**「高貴な、気高い」

4 **memoir**「回顧録、回想録」

7 **rhetorical**「修辞的な、修辞効果を狙った」

8 **House of Commons**「庶民院」イギリスの下院にあたる議会で、現在の定数は 650 人。上院にあたる貴族院（House of Lords）と両院制を構成している。

9 **in gratitude for ~**「～に感謝して」

9 **Royal Air Force**「王立空軍」イギリス空軍とも表記される。1918 年に世界で初めての空軍として独立した。RAF という略称でも知られる。

11 **Luftwaffe**「ドイツ国防軍空軍」ナチス政権下における空軍を主に差す。

12 **Battle of Britain**「ブリテンの戦い」1940 年 7 月 10 日～ 10 月 31 日までに行われたドイツ軍の大空襲とそれを迎え撃ったイギリス空軍の戦い。イギリスが勝利し、ドイツ軍の本土侵略を防いだ。

14 **oft** = often　本文にある oft-quoted（よく引用される）のように複合語で用いられる。

16 **adverb**「副詞」

38

An interesting variation of this use of "so" is provided in the British poet Alfred 20
Tennyson's hugely admired long poem "In Memoriam A.H.H.", which was
published in 1850. Tennyson wrote it as a requiem for his beloved friend Arthur
Henry Hallam (the "A.H.H." of the title), who had died suddenly and tragically at
the age of 22, and the poem is said to have been a great comfort to Queen Victoria
years later when she was grieving over the death of her husband, Prince Albert. 25
The variation here of the use of "so" occurs in lines that are still often quoted
today in the English-speaking world: "So many worlds, so much to do, / So little
done, such things to be." Each "so" here is being used for special emphasis on the
extremity of a condition, and no matter how it might be translated "poetically"
into Japanese, in ordinary writing and conversation it expresses something like 30
"*amarinimo*" (あまりにも). In that sense, this "so" carries the implication of "over-
whelmingness" and might almost be rephrased as "Too many worlds, too much to
do, / Too little done …."

Anyone who has taught "Writing in English" to university students in Japan
will undoubtedly have found one of the students' most misused vocabulary items 35
to be this tiny adverb "so." It is most often misused by them as a kind of substitute
for "very." One example of this would be the following strange sentence: "I think
that there are so many nice shirts, so I will choose one." Some English textbooks
employed in Japanese secondary schools also misuse "so" in the same way.

While this kind of "so" can, indeed, be used for emphasis, as in "I'm so tired!" 40
(in the sense of "*amarinimo tsukareteiru*!" 〈あまりにも疲れている〉), such a usage is
really an abbreviation of the "… so + adjective + that …." form, e.g., "I was so
tired that I couldn't even stand up," which indicates a specific extent or degree. An
abbreviated form like "I'm so tired!" simply leaves the implied specific degree or
extent up to the imagination of the reader or listener. It is important to remember 45
that this usage of "so" is essentially an exclamatory form, which is why it is most
appropriately followed in writing by an exclamation point (!).

NOTES

20 **Alfred Tennyson**「アルフレッド・テニスン」(1809–1892) 英リンカンシャーで、牧師の
子として生まれる。ケンブリッジ大学在学中から詩作をはじめる。1850 年ウィリアム・
ワーズワースのあとを受けて桂冠詩人となり、1884 年には男爵に叙せられる。

22 **requiem**「レクイエム、鎮魂歌 (詩)」

43 **degree**「程度、度合い」

44 **leave ~ up to …**「～を…にまかせる」

46 **exclamatory**「感嘆表現の」

There actually is, however, a limited idiomatic use of "so" in which it does function as a kind of substitute for "very." The most commonly seen example of such an idiomatic usage is the phrase "Thank you so much (for …)." This simply 50 means the same thing as "Thank you very much (for …)," and further emphasis is, in fact, often given by writing or saying "Thank you so very much (for …)."

Finally, let us consider why "I think that there are so many nice shirts …." is an example of misuse. The intended meaning was undoubtedly "I think that there are very many nice shirts, and I will choose one," but to an ordinary non-Japanese 55 reader of English, the "so" of "so many" here would appear to be being used to express the opinion "*amarinimo (ōi)*（あまりにも〔多い〕)," which is quite different from "very (many)" and would be significantly confusing.

Exercises

*F*ill in the *B*lanks

日本語を参考に（　）に so か very を入れてそれぞれの英文を完成させよう。

1. 彼女の新しい小説はとてもいいものになる、と私たちは思っている。

   We believe her new novel will be (　　　) good.

2. ジェーンはあまりにも美しい！

   Jane is (　　　) beautiful!

3. 私の家からとても近いところにいい喫茶店があったが、新型コロナウイルスの大流行のせいで閉店してしまっている。

   There was a nice coffee shop (　　　) close to my place, but it has been closed because of the COVID-19 pandemic .

4. 高校の数学が、ここまで高度になっているとは知らなかった。

I had had no idea that mathematics in high school had become (　　　　　　)
advanced.

5. そんなに心配しなくてもいいよ。

You don't need to worry (　　　　　　) much.

Translate into Japanese

以下の名言を和訳してみよう。

1. Alone we can do so little; together we can do so much. (Helen Keller)

....
....
....

2. Of all men's miseries the bitterest is this: to know so much and to have control over nothing. (Herodotus)

....
....
....

3. Success is to be measured not so much by the position that one has reached in life as by the obstacles which he has overcome. (Booker T. Washington)

....
....
....

Translate into **E**nglish

以下の文を英訳してみよう。

1. 昨日は、アスファルトが溶けてしまうほど暑かった。（so 〜 that を使って）

   ....
   ....
   ....

2. 彼は、あなたが思っているほど無知な人間ではない。実際、非常に知的で有能な人物だ。
   （so を使って）

   ....
   ....
   ....
   ....

3. いまだかつてこれほど長く続き、そして、これほど広範囲にわたる洪水が起きたことは
   なかった。（so を使って）

   ....
   ....
   ....

Lesson **8** 性的に中立な表現を考える

Gender-neutral Expressions

過去半世紀の間、女性や性的マイノリティの当然の権利が拡大されるなか、性的区別をなくした表現が作られてきた。それは、従来の英語の語彙と文法にも影響を与えている。この間、英語圏で非難の的になってきた he や she、そして stewardess, waitress など男女別の代名詞・名詞はどのように変化してきたのだろうか？

Grammatical Points

- he や waitress など性を特定する代名詞・名詞を使わずに、性的に中立な表現を使って英語を書く方法とは？
- actress, fireman, Mr., Mrs. など一方の性を表す語が、今どのような言い換えをされているのか？

Vocabulary Check

以下の単語の定義を下から選び、その番号を〔　　〕に入れよう。

aesthetically 〔　　〕	awkward 〔　　〕	default 〔　　〕
employment 〔　　〕	irrelevant 〔　　〕	ubiquitous 〔　　〕

1. not related to a particular situation or issue—and therefore not meaningful with regard to it
2. not smooth or graceful, creating a feeling of clumsiness
3. from the viewpoint of beauty or attractiveness
4. the use of something for a specific purpose
5. seeming to be found or to exist everywhere
6. a standard setting in a computer program or other mechanism

Gender-neutral Expressions

22 With rising awareness of the identity-issues faced by members of the LGBTQ community, greater stress has, in recent years, been put on the use of gender-neutral (often called "gender-inclusive") expressions in English. Most of the controversy in this area has revolved around how to deal with forms of English's gender-specific personal "she" and "he." A problem often arises, for example, in 5 cases in which gender is irrelevant, as in a sentence like this: "No one is allowed to vote for [himself?] [herself?]."

For many people, a combined-expression like "himself/herself" in such a sentence would be aesthetically unpleasant to look at, while use of "or," as in "herself or himself," would feel stylistically awkward. A large portion of those 10 people would also be likely to find the increasingly popular use of "they" as a singular pronoun, as in "A citizen should exercise their right to vote," to simply "feel wrong," and they would never think of writing "No one is allowed to vote for *themself*."

While that has been the situation with pronouns, regarding the elimination of 15 unnecessarily gender-specific nouns, such as "actress," "fireman," "chairman," "stewardess," or "waitress," there has, fortunately, been much less controversy. Most people find little to object to in referring to a female film star as an "actor," nor do they find anything especially offensive in the use of gender-neutral terms like "firefighter," "chairperson," "flight attendant," or "server." 20

Learners of English who have an interest in this subject might find a useful

NOTES ─────────

1 **LGBTQ**「性的少数者」lesbian, gay, bisexual, transgender, queer の頭文字から。Q は questioning を表すことも（つまり、自己の性的指向を明確に決定していないことを指す）。
2 **gender-neutral**「性別による区別のない、性的に中立な」
3 **gender-inclusive**「性差を抱合した、性差のない」
4 **controversy**「論争、議論」
4 **revolve around ~**「～を中心議題として展開する」
5 **personal**「人称の」
12 **singular**「単数の」
15 **elimination**「撤廃、廃止、除去」
20 **server**「給仕人」以前は、waiter と waitress を用い男女で使い分けていたが、現在では、性別を特定しないこの語を使うことが一般化している。

44

resource in the United Nations' "Guidelines for gender-inclusive language in English." While these well-balanced guidelines were produced specifically for the benefit of United Nations staff, they can be usefully employed by the general public, as well, in business communications, academic writing, and even ordinary 25 email correspondence.

23 As examples of replacing gender-specific expressions with ones that are gender inclusive, the UN guidelines recommend, for instance, using "staffing shortages" in place of "manpower shortages" and using "artificial" or "human-caused" in place of "man-made." With respect to issues regarding pronoun usage, they 30 recommend using the vocabulary items "one" or "who," offering these example sentences:

"A staff member in Antarctica earns less than he would in New York."
↓
"A staff member in Antarctica earns less than one in New York."

"If a complainant is not satisfied with the board's decision, he can ask for a 35 rehearing."
↓
"A complainant who is not satisfied with the board's decision can ask for a rehearing.

The guidelines also note the potential helpfulness of switching from singular to plural, as in this way: 40

"A substitute judge must certify that he has familiarized himself with the record of the proceedings."
↓

NOTES
22 **resource**「(資料などの) 供給源、資源」
22 **United Nations' "Guidelines … in English"** https://www.un.org/en/gender-inclusive-language/guidelines.shtml を参照。
26 **correspondence**「文書のやりとり、通信」
28 **shortage**「不足」
33 **Antarctica**「南極大陸」
35 **complainant**「原告」
36 **rehearing**「再審理」
40 **plural**「複数の」

"Substitute judges must certify that they have familiarized themselves with the record of the proceedings."

Another interesting issue often raised is the use of the gender-specific honorifics 45 "Mister" or "Miss." The first appearance in relatively recent times of *serious* objections to the way they were being used were those regarding the double-standard that is obvious in the contrast between "Mrs." and "Mr." Specifically, "Mrs." makes it clear that a person is legally married, while "Mr." leaves marital status unclear. Use of the honorific "Ms." as a way to avoid this double-standard 50 first began to gain widespread popularity with the founding, in 1971, of *Ms.*, America's first nationally distributed feminist magazine. Since then, "Ms." has gradually become the default honorific for use with either the family name or the full name of a woman, and its use is particularly ubiquitous in the business world.

This change has not, however, satisfied many persons who identify as being 55 "non-binary," since both "Mr." and "Ms." are gender-specific. For them, the gender-neutral term "Mx." is most often the preferred choice, and "Mx." has, over the years, gained a limited degree of currency. With regard to such employment of the letter "x" as kind of placeholder, similar to what is known in the software world as a "wildcard character," it is interesting to note the far wider general 60 acceptance of its use in another neologism in American English: "Latinx." Until the appearance of "Latinx" in the early 2000s, the gender-specific terms "Latina" (female) and "Latino" (male) were the most widely accepted for reference to people in the United States who had Latin American roots or an ethnic identity that was Latin American. 65

Actually, a large number of those who identify as "non-binary" insist on use of the abbreviation "LGBTQN" (still others, ones who feel that their own identities do not fall within any of those categories, insist on "LGBTQN+").

NOTES

49 **marital status**「結婚歴、配偶者の有無」
50 **honorific**「敬称」
56 **non-binary**「自らを女性・男性のどちらでもないと認識している」
58 **currency**「流布、流通」
59 **placeholder**「プレースホルダー」文章や図の入力の際、後から挿入することを想定して、確保された場所や空間。
61 **neologism**「造語、新語」

Exercises

*R*evise the *E*xpressions

アンダーラインの付いた単語を、現在の視点でより適切な表現に言い換えてみよう。

1. She is <u>fat</u> and ought to go on a diet.　　［　　　　　　　　　］

2. My daughter and her friends are planning a special dinner for <u>old people</u> next week.　　　　　　　　　　［　　　　　　　　　］

3. When I was traveling in Arizona, I met a number of <u>Indians</u>.
　　　　　　　　　　　　　　　　［　　　　　　　　　］

4. The other day, while I was riding my bicycle, I was stopped by two <u>policemen</u> and had my bike inspected.　　　　［　　　　　　　　　］

5. One of the basic skills a <u>salesman</u> must have is the ability to clearly introduce products and services to customers.　　［　　　　　　　　　］

*T*ranslate into *J*apanese

次の名言を和訳してみよう。

1. Both men and women should feel free to be sensitive. Both men and women should feel free to be strong. It is time that we all perceived gender as a spectrum instead of two sets of opposing ideals. We should stop defining each other by what we are not and start defining ourselves by who we are.

(Emma Watson)

....
....
....
....
....

2. I've never met a gay person who regretted coming out – including myself. Life at last begins to make sense, when you are open and honest. (Ian McKellen)

   ....

   ....

   ....

3. Society as whole benefits immeasurably from a climate in which all persons, regardless of race or gender, may have the opportunity to earn respect, responsibility, advancement, and remuneration based on ability.

   (Sandra Day O'Connor)

   ....

   ....

   ....

   ....

Translate into English

以下の文を英訳してみよう。

1. 1970年代からアメリカでは、人種差別、男女差別の根絶を目標に、様々な新しい表現が考え出され、使用されてきている。

   ....

   ....

2. 「政治的に正しい」とされる表現は、性別、人種、職業、宗教、病名、生物の名前まで多岐に及んでいる。

   ....

   ....

3. 政治的に正しい表現は人々の意識を確実に変えてきたが、「表現の自由」を盾に、SNSで反論を展開し世論を煽る者もいる。

   ....

   ....

   ....

Lesson 9 コンマと事実

Commas and Facts

"Penn's daughter Margaret ...." と "Penn's daughter, Margaret, ..." のような英文における
コンマの用法を考えたことがあるだろうか？ コンマの有無は、関係代名詞の限定（制限）用
法と非限定（非制限）用法と同様の意味を伝えることができ、文章を書く際に正確な事実を
伝える決め手になる場合がある。日本語の句読法とも異なるコンマの用法を考えてみよう。

Grammatical Points

- 英語におけるコンマの限定（制限）用法と非限定（非制限）用法
- コンマの有無で伝えることができる事実

Vocabulary Check

以下の単語の定義を下から選び、その番号を ［　］に入れよう。

accurate ［　］	attribute ［　］	distinguish ［　］
offspring ［　］	rigorous ［　］	sibling ［　］

1. a brother or sister
2. detailed, careful, and sometimes physically demanding
3. someone's child or children
4. correct in all details
5. to recognize or indicate the difference between two people or things
6. regard something as the result of a particular thing

Commas and Facts

25

The best American magazine of general cultural interest is, by far, *The New Yorker*. It has been in publication since 1925, and the consistently high quality of the writing that appears in its pages can mainly be attributed to three factors: it publishes fiction and non-fiction articles by only the very best writers (and pays those writers very well), it employs talented editors who enforce strict 5 standards of prose quality, and it also has a rigorous "fact-checking department" whose specialists carefully comb through each piece of writing to make sure that anything expressed as a "fact" is, in fact, a "fact."

One particularly well-done "Anniversary Issue" of *The New Yorker* included a long and truly fascinating article on the process of fact-checking ("Checkpoints," 10 *The New Yorker*, Feb. 9 & 16, 2009). This article was written by John McPhee, a well-known author of non-fiction books and a long-time staff writer at the magazine. In it, McPhee tells a story that illustrates the potential importance of punctuation in the accuracy of English.

In a book he had been writing about the history of fishing in the United States, 15 he had described the interest in fishing that was shown by a certain young woman, Margaret Penn, whose father, William Penn (1644–1718), had founded both the city of Philadelphia and the colony of Pennsylvania. The need for fact checking arose in the following sentence: "Penn's daughter Margaret fished in the Delaware [River] ...." The problem, as McPhee described it, was: "Should there be commas 20 around Margaret or no commas around Margaret?" That is, should the sentence be as written above, or should it be written as "Penn's daughter, Margaret, fished in the Delaware, ..."?

NOTES

1 *The New Yorker*「ニューヨーカー」1925 年 2 月に創刊された雑誌。ニューヨーク市で催されるイベントなどの文化的な情報のほかに、ルポルタージュ、小説、詩、風刺漫画などが掲載されている。村上春樹の短編小説の英訳が掲載されることでも知られる。
2 **consistently**「一貫して、矛盾なく」
5 **enforce**「守らせる、強制する」
6 **prose**「散文（韻を踏んでいない文章）」
7 **comb through**「厳密にチェックする」
10 **fascinating**「興味深い」
14 **punctuation**「句読法」
18 **colony**「植民地」

Why should this be a problem? McPhee continues: "The presence or absence of commas would, in effect, say whether Penn had one daughter or more than one. The commas—there or missing there—were not just commas; they were facts, …." McPhee needed to make sure of the nature of Penn's offspring in order to know how to punctuate the sentence so that it would be factually accurate. In the end, he explains, "Margaret, one of Penn's several daughters, went into the book without commas."

The use of commas in a construction like "Penn's daughter, Margaret, fished in the Delaware, …." is the same as if they were being used in a non-restrictive relative clause, such as "The boy, who was Japanese, won the piano competition." Since the commas in this sentence indicate that the clause "who was Japanese" is simply giving parenthetical information about the boy and is not being used to limit his identity to one boy among other possible boys, the sentence indicates that there is only one boy at issue here. If, on the other hand, there were no commas, i.e., if the sentence were "The boy who was Japanese won the piano competition," it would express some very different facts—that there had been two or more boys in the competition, that only one of those boys had been Japanese, and that this Japanese boy had won.

In the same way, when a proper noun is used in apposition to a common noun, commas surrounding the proper noun would indicate non-restriction, non-limitation. Let us consider, for example, a situation in which a female student happened to be writing about the children in the family in which she had been raised, which had included two boys and two girls. In order to be factually accurate, she would write "I seldom played with my sister, Aya, during my teenage years," using commas because she has only ever had one sister and there is no need to distinguish that sister from any other sister.

Conversely, in reference to one of her two brothers, she would write "I seldom

NOTES

27 **the nature of**~「～の実態、～がどのような状況にあるか」
28 **punctuate**「句読点を付ける」
28 **factually**「事実に照らして」
32 **non-restrictive relative clause**「非限定［非制限］関係詞節」
35 **parenthetical**「カッコでくくられた、補足的な」
38 **i.e.**「すなわち（ラテン語より）」
42 **proper noun**「固有名詞」後続の common noun は「普通名詞」
42 **in apposition to**~「～と同格で」
50 **in reference to**~「～に関して」

played with my brother Ryō during my teenage years," using no commas, which would be factually correct, for since she had more than one brother, there was a need to limit the identity of this particular "my brother" to that of a single person. That is, in order not to mislead a reader on that account, she would need to use a restrictive form. 55

Perhaps, in real life, no one would care very much if a sentence about a student's own family happened to be factually inaccurate with respect to the number of her/his male or female siblings, but the publisher of a factually inaccurate sentence about someone as famous as William Penn could expect to receive a flood of complaints. 60

NOTES

60 **a flood of ~**「大量の～」

Exercises

*P*ut the *W*ords into the *C*orrect *O*rder

日本語を参考に、必要ならコンマを加えて、(　　　　　) 内の単語を並び替えて正しい英文にしてみよう。(文頭は大文字に変えてください)

1. 健太の犬のジャックはダックスフントだ。(健太は、一匹しか飼っていない)

....

(dachshund / dog / is / Kenta's / Jack / a)

2. リサの犬のロキシーは、ポメラニアン種だ。(リサは、複数の犬を飼っている)

....

(is / Pomeranian / Roxy / Risa's / dog / a)

3. スマートフォンを持っていた社員はすぐに会社に電話をした。（みなスマートフォンを持っていた）

....

....

（immediately / carrying / called / the employees / office / their / smartphones）

4. 外国語を全く知らないアメリカ人（だけ）は、再教育されるべきだ。

....

....

(ignorant / foreign / Americans / should / of / languages / re-educated / be)

Translate into Japanese

次の名言を和訳してみよう。

1. Facts do not cease to exist because they are ignored. (Aldous Huxley)

....

....

2. The degree of one's emotions varies inversely with one's knowledge of the facts. (Bertrand Russell)

....

....

3. You can never get all the facts from just one newspaper, and unless you have all the facts, you cannot make proper judgements about what is going on.

(Harry S. Truman)

....

....

....

Translate into English

以下の文を非限定（非制限）用法のコンマを使って英訳してみよう。

1. 私の姉の京子は、生涯結婚しなかった。（一人しか姉はいない）

   ....
   ....

2. ロンドン出身の最も有名な俳優の一人であるマイケル・ケインは、コックニー訛_{なまり}で知られている。

   ....
   ....
   ....

3. 午前6時に台風による注意報が発令された。会社からメールで連絡を受けた社員は、自宅で待機した。（社員は全員メールで連絡を受けた）

   ....
   ....
   ....

Lesson 10 since と because を使いこなす

Since I Don't Have You

現在完了形と一緒に学ぶことが多い接続詞の since、そして、中学一年からおなじみの because。どちらも用法によって同様の意味をもつ場合があるが、単純に入れ替えはできない。二つの基本接続詞の意味を確認しながら、英語の因果関係について考えてみよう。

Grammatical Points

- since と because の意味と用法
- 因果関係に従って適切な接続詞を選ぶ方法

Vocabulary Check

以下の単語の定義を下から選び、その番号を 〔　　〕に入れよう。

ambiguity 〔　　〕	equivalent 〔　　〕	feature 〔　　〕
fund 〔　　〕	sloppy 〔　　〕	solicit 〔　　〕

1. careless, inexact
2. to provide money for a particular purpose
3. to ask someone for something, especially money, information, or help
4. the quality of being open to different interpretations
5. to include a particular person or thing as an important part of something
6. basically the same in value, amount, function, meaning, etc.

Since I Don't Have You

In United States television, the closest equivalent to Japan's NHK is the Public Broadcasting Service (PBS), which offers U.S. viewers a wide range of high-quality news, education, entertainment, and culturally-related programming. PBS is officially an NPO that has more than 350 "member television stations," many of which are owned by universities. 5

Unlike NHK, PBS is not funded by license fees. It has many outside sources of financial support, but it also needs to solicit donations from private citizens through regularly scheduled pledge drives. These drives are occasionally quite financially successful, culturally influential, and historically significant. One especially remarkable example of this phenomenon was a special program 10 produced for a pledge drive conducted by the member station WQED-TV in Pittsburgh, Pennsylvania. It was a videotaped live-performance show entitled "Doo Wop 50" and broadcast on December 5, 1999. It raised more than $20 million in donations, the most of any pledge-drive special in the history of PBS to that time.

"Doo Wop 50" was "culturally influential and historically significant" for 15 its important contribution to the revival of interest in and love for the musical genre known as "doo wop." The revived interest and love, which continue to be conspicuous even today, were initially sparked by Rhino Records' 1994 release of the 4-CD box set *Doo Wop Box*, which is said to have been the original inspiration for the production of "Doo Wop 50." 20

Both the box set and "Doo Wop 50" feature a song that has become one of the most beloved of all in the genre, "Since I Don't Have You" by the Skyliners. A hit

NOTES————————

4 **NPO**「特定非営利活動法人」（Nonprofit Organization の略）
6 **license fees**「受信料」
7 **donation**「寄付、助成」
8 **pledge drive**「資金集めのためのキャンペーン」
8 **occasionally**「時々、たまに」
12 **Doo Wop** → doo-wop「ドゥー・ワップ」1950 年代に米国で流行したリズム・アンド・ブルースのグループ・コーラス。
13 **raise**「資金を集める・調達する」
18 **conspicuous**「顕著な、際立った」
18 **Rhino Records**「ライノ・レコード」米ワーナー・ミュージック傘下のレコード・レーベル。過去音源の企画盤・再発盤を多く手掛けている。

single in 1958, this song has been heavily covered over the years by artists ranging
from Art Garfunkel to Guns N' Roses. The most amazing of all cover versions of
"Since I Don't Have You" appeared in 1998 on the Brian Setzer Orchestra's *The* 25
Dirty Boogie, that extraordinary swing band's third album.

The opening lyrics of this song offer learners of English an interesting example
of potential ambiguity in use of the language: "I don't have plans and schemes /
and I don't have hopes and dreams / I don't have anything / since I don't have
you." The "potential ambiguity" here arises from the use of the word "since," 30
which, as English-Japanese dictionaries usually tell their users, can mean either
"… *no yue ni* (…のゆえに), … *dakara* (…だから)" or "… *irai* (…以来), … *ikō* (…以降)."
Does the singer mean that he/she has no "hopes and dreams" because of having
lost "you" or, rather, has had no "hopes and dreams" since the time of losing "you"?

Naturally, if the intended meaning is the latter, a "grammatically precise" 35
writing would be "I haven't had hopes and dreams since I haven't had you," but
the lyrics to popular songs are only rarely "grammatically precise." They are much
more often highly "conversational" and "grammatically sloppy," and the usual
interpretation of "since" in this song is, actually, the latter. One reason for that is
the "timing" expressed in the final lines of the lyrics: "When you walked out on 40
me / in walked old Misery / and he's been here since then."

30

Such ambiguity often presents itself in the writing in English of Japanese
university students, too. Consider, for instance, the following typical sentence
written by a male student:

NOTES ────────────────

23 **range from ~ to …**「〜から…に及ぶ範囲で」

24 **Art Garfunkel**「アート・ガーファンクル」(1941–) 米ニューヨーク出身の歌手。1964 年
にポール・サイモンとサイモン＆ガーファンクルを結成し、数々のヒット曲を出す。70 年
に活動停止した後は、ソロとして活動。

24 **Guns N' Roses**「ガンズ＆ローゼズ」1985 年にロサンゼルスで結成されたハード・ロッ
ク・バンド。アクセル・ローズ（ヴォーカル）、スラッシュ（ギター）らが中心メンバー。
メンバーの脱退・復帰を経て、現在も活動を続ける。

25 **Brian Setzer Orchestra**　ニューヨーク州出身のギタリストでシンガーのブライアン・セ
ッツァー (1959–) が率いるビッグバンド。ジャズとロックを融合させた「スウィング・ロ
ック」を中心とした音楽を展開。アルバム『ダーティ・ブギ』(The Dirty Boogie) は、大
ヒットを記録し、グラミー賞も 2 部門受賞している。

26 **extraordinary**「並外れた、非凡な」

39 **interpretation**「解釈」

41 **in walked old Misery**　歌詞のため倒置されている。old Misery walked in が通常の語順。

"Since my father died 14 years ago, my mother single-handedly raised three 45
children, including me."

The problem here also stems from use of a "Since ...," clause; one cannot tell whether the "Since" is being used to indicate a span of time or to indicate causality. If it is meant to indicate a span of time up to the present, for example, the sentence needs to be corrected to "Since my father died 14 years ago, my 50 mother has single-handedly raised ...." If the mother is no longer raising any children, on the other hand, it should be corrected to something like "After my father died 14 years ago, my mother single-handedly raised ...."

By way of contrast, if the "Since ..." clause was meant to indicate a "cause-and-effect" relationship, as in "Because my father died 14 years ago, ...", the fact that 55 the death was "14 years ago" would not be causally relevant, and the fact that the number of children was "three" would not be an effect of the death. In this case, the sentence should be rewritten as:

"My father died 14 years ago, and after that [since then], my mother single-handedly raised [has single-handedly raised] three children, including me." 60

NOTES——————————————————

49 **causality**「因果関係」

Exercises

*R*evise the *S*entences

以下の文を、論理的に正しい文、より自然な文に直してみよう。

1. Ever since Ken won the lottery, his family is bickering among themselves every day.

   ....
   ....
   ....

2. I do listen to the music of BTS, but that is not simply since it has become popular among some of my friends.

....
....
....

3. Jeff has seemed to be another person because he got married.

....
....

4. They haven't been able to play soccer after their ball rolled into the river and was washed away.

....
....
....

5. I think music theory is very important for pianists. Because it will help them improvise and compose music more easily.

....
....
....

Translate into Japanese

次の名言を和訳してみよう。

1. Since a politician never believes what he says, he is quite surprised to be taken at his word. (Charles de Gaulle)

....
....
....

2. Opportunity is missed by most people because it is dressed in overalls and looks like work. (Thomas A. Edison)

....
....
....

3. Laughter and tears are both responses to frustration and exhaustion. I myself prefer to laugh, since there is less cleaning up to do afterward. (Kurt Vonnegut)

....
....
....

Translate into English

以下の文を英訳してみよう。

1. 彼女は「今夜は髪を洗わないといけないから、映画には行けない」と言ったが、それは単なる口実だと思う。

....
....
....

2. イチローが引退してからというもの、私の父は野球に興味を持てない日々を送っている。

....
....
....

3. なぜ人は、政治家に騙され続けるのだろうか？　それは、人間が真実より、嘘に魅力を感じるからかもしれない。

....
....
....

Lesson **11** 1つだけではない only の意味と用法

That's All He Did

Thurber

Writings & Drawings

英語学習者なら誰でも知っている only だが、文中に置かれる位置によって、文の意味を変える働きをもつ。また、「〜だけ」＝ only と機械的に記憶されているために、英語のリアリティとはかけ離れた英語表現が作られてしまうこともある。おなじみの基本副詞 only に焦点をあてることによって見えてくる、英語の論理にせまってみよう。

Grammatical Points

- 位置によって変わる only の用法
- 「〜だけ」「〜のみ」を表す英語の副詞について考える

Vocabulary Check

以下の単語の定義を下から選び、その番号を ［　　］ に入れよう。

appropriate ［　　］	assume ［　　］	encounter ［　　］
purist ［　　］	satirical ［　　］	subsequent ［　　］

1. to meet someone or something unexpectedly
2. using exaggeration or irony in a humorous way to expose or criticize someone's or something's faults
3. someone who insists on the exact following of traditional rules, especially in language or style
4. suitable or proper for the particular circumstances
5. suppose something to be true without having proof of it
6. happening or coming after something in time

That's All He Did

31

Among the several literary prizes annually awarded in the United States, the relatively new Thurber Prize for American Humor (first awarded in 1997) is one that many people look forward to each year with special interest. It was established in honor of the great American humorist, cartoonist, author, playwright, and journalist James Thurber by the nonprofit literary arts center known as Thurber 5 House. This center is located in Columbus, Ohio, in Thurber's childhood home, which is listed on the National Register of Historic Places.

In his stories, Thurber tended to write about the frustrations and irritations commonly encountered by ordinary people in their daily lives, as well as about the various eccentricities such otherwise perfectly ordinary people often exhibited. 10 One of Thurber's many enduringly popular books is *The Owl in the Attic and Other Perplexities*, which was first published in 1931. In addition to humorous stories, the book also contains a very entertaining satirical essay entitled "Ladies' and Gentlemen's Guide to Modern English Usage."

Here, from that essay, is a short passage that deals with the issue of where 15 to locate the word "only" in a sentence, a subject that should be of interest to Japanese learners of the language:

The purist will say that the expression: 'He only died last week' is incorrect, and that it should be: 'He died only last week.' The purist's contention is that the first sentence, if carried out to a natural conclusion, would give us 20 something like this: "He only *died* last week, he didn't do anything else, that's

---

NOTES

3 **be established in honor of ~**「～をたたえて創設される」

4 **cartoonist**（新聞などに載る）「風刺漫画家」

5 **James Thurber**「ジェームズ・サーバー」(1894–1961) 米オハイオ州出身の作家、漫画家、劇作家。*The New Yorker* を中心に活躍。短編小説 *The Secret Life of Walter Mitty*（『ウォルター・ミティの秘密の生活』）などの多数の作品ある。

7 **National Register of Historic Places**「アメリカ合衆国国家歴史登録財」建築物、史跡などを対象にした、米政府による文化遺産保護制度。

10 **eccentricities** → eccentricity「風変わりな行動、奇行」

10 **exhibit**「表に出す、見せる」

11 **enduringly**「永続的に、後世に残って」

19 **contention**「論点、主張」

all he did." It isn't a natural conclusion, however, because nobody would say that ….

32   What Thurber means here by "nobody would say that" is that there would never be a situation in which such a statement would be appropriate. That is, in Thurber's 25 view, it is essentially impossible to imagine a case in which a person *only* did *one* thing during an entire week: he *died*, and that was *the only thing he did* that week.

  Learners of English do, however, often create actual problems in their writing by mislocating the word "only." When correcting the writing in English by *Japanese* learners, native-speakers of English are likely to encounter such sentences 30 as "Only I want to say is our salaries are too low." If those native-speakers happen to have had only very limited experience in such correction work, they might easily misunderstand the intention of the writer here to have been "I am the only person who wants to say that our salaries are too low." Someone with *extensive* previous experience, though, would immediately assume that the intended 35 meaning had actually been "The only thing I want to say is that our salaries are too low."

  A more common problem comes with a sentence like "They only succeeded on the first day." The first impression one would get from this sentence is that it was intended to mean "The first day was the only day on which they succeeded." 40 Subsequent reading, however, might well suggest that in fact it had been meant to say "They were the only ones who succeeded on the first day." Because there is the possibility of seriously problematic ambiguity in such a sentence construction, some language "purists" find acceptable only those sentences in which "only" is placed *directly before the word or phrase it is meant to modify.* 45

33   For learners who want to be on the safe side, the rule of the "purists" mentioned by Thurber can always be safely followed. Specifically, rather than writing, for example, "She only wants the most expensive wine on the list," which is superficially ambiguous, they can write either "She wants only the most expensive wine on the list" or "Only she wants the most expensive wine on the list," 50

NOTES
34 **extensive** 「広範囲にわたる」
43 **sentence construction** 「文の組み立て、文の構成」
45 **modify** 「修飾する」
49 **superficially** 「表面上、一見」

depending on which of the meanings they want to convey. But it is important to remember that, in *ordinary* writing, "She only wants the most expensive wine on the list" would naturally be interpreted to mean "She wants only the most expensive wine on the list." Also, if the idea of "Only *she* wants the most expensive wine on the list" were to be expressed by putting a modifier *between* 55 "She" and "wants," that modifier would ordinarily not be "only;" it would be "alone," as in "She alone wants the most expensive wine on the list."

This sort of use of "alone" is also often preferable for an ambiguously written sentence such as "We can adjust the frequency by only controlling the input data selector," which probably should be rewritten as "We are able to adjust the 60 frequency simply by controlling the input data selector alone."

NOTES

55 **modifier**「修飾語」
59 **frequency**「周波数」

Exercises

*F*ill in the *B*lanks

以下の文の「だけ」に注目して、(　　　　) 内に単語を 1 語入れよう。

1. 私は東京にいるときだけ、花粉症になる。

   I get hay fever (　　　　　) when I am in Tokyo.

2. 一匹の犬だけでも、かなりの世話が必要になる。

   Even a single dog (　　　　　) requires quite lot of care.

3. その殺人犯のことを考えただけで、震えがくる。

   The (　　　　　) thought of the murderer makes me shiver.

4. ビリーはピアノの調律をする<u>だけ</u>で、めったに弾かない。

   Billy (　　　　　　) tunes pianos; he rarely plays any.

5. ただ、君に会いたかった<u>だけ</u>なんだ。

   It's (　　　　　　) I wanted to see you.

Translate into Japanese

次の名言を和訳してみよう。

1. There is only one corner of the universe you can be certain of improving, and that's your own self. (Aldous Huxley)

   ....

   ....

   ....

2. We're born alone, we live alone, we die alone. Only through our love and friendship can we create the illusion for the moment that we're not alone.

   (Orson Welles)

   ....

   ....

   ....

3. Sometimes the majority just means all the fools are on the same side.

   (John F. Kennedy)

   ....

   ....

   ....

Translate into English

以下の文を英訳してみよう。

1. 大量解雇。それが彼が社長在任中に行った唯一の業績だった。

   ....
   ....
   ....

2. ウクライナ戦争で一人息子を亡くした女性についてのニュース報道を見て、もらい泣き
   してしまった。

   ....
   ....
   ....

3. 「お一人様でございますか？」
   「はい、一人です」

   ....
   ....
   ....

Lesson **12** 「の」を表す in と of の違い

The Turn
in the Weather

大恐慌時代に公開された映画『トップ・ハット』。この映画は大不況に苦しむアメリカ人にとって娯楽を提供するだけでなく、ミュージカル映画の傑作として、現在まで多くのファンを魅了している。この映画の挿入歌 "Isn't This a Lovely Day?" の歌詞の一節、The turn in the weather の英語に使われた前置詞の意味を考えてみよう。

*G*rammatical *P*oints

- 日本語の「AのB」を表すとき用いる前置詞は of でいいのだろうか？
- 過去時制における now, current, contemporary などの訳し方

*V*ocabulary *C*heck

以下の単語の定義を下から選び、その番号を ［　　］ に入れよう。

bleak ［　］	deliberately ［　］	fortuitously ［　　］
masculinity ［　　］	render ［　　］	solace ［　］

1. to cause someone or something to be in a particular state or condition
2. characteristics that are traditionally considered to be typical of men
3. luckily, fortunately
4. not hopeful or encouraging
5. comfort or consolation in a time of grief or anxiety
6. intentionally, in a way that was intended or planned

The Turn *in* the Weather

During the terrible worldwide Great Depression of the1930s, unemployment in the U.S. reached roughly 23%, and no social safety net had yet been created for its citizens. Large numbers of them could not even afford food, and, shockingly, some Americans, including children, actually starved to death. In times as frightening as these, many people naturally sought out some source of solace and hope. And for 5 it, they often looked to the entertainment that was available to them then. Variety programs on the radio were an important diversion, of course, but for something to *watch*, not simply to *listen to*, *movies* were everything (television did not become generally available until after WWII).

Movie tickets in those days were still inexpensive enough to be affordable 10 for most people, and Hollywood producers soon discovered that what the public most desired was *escapist* entertainment. People wanted something that would help them forget, even for a short time, the bleak reality of their daily lives, and Hollywood was ready to provide it. Further, in a fortuitously timed technical advancement, films were no longer "silent"—the age of "all-talkies" had arrived. 15 Movies were now able to compete with radio by offering not only listenable conversation but *music* as well. And the music best designed to lift the spirit of the nation was that which had the bright, happy beat of the current "Jazz Age." Thus began the first Golden Age of the *movie musical*.

Among the countless movie musicals produced in that era, the most perfectly 20

NOTES

1 **Great Depression**「大恐慌」1929 年 10 月の米ニューヨーク市場の暴落をきっかけに発生した世界的大不況。1930 年代後半まで続いた。

1 **unemployment**「失業、失業者数」

5 **sought out** → seek out「探し出す、見つけ出す」

6 **look to**「期待する、待望する」

7 **diversion**「気晴らし、娯楽」

9 **WWII** = World War II「第二次世界大戦 (1939~45)」the Second World War とも言う。

12 **escapist**「現実逃避的な」

15 **silent**「無声の」ここではサイレント（無声）映画のこと。

15 **all-talkies**「すべてトーキー」talkie は talking picure の略語で、サイレント映画に対して、映像と音声が同期した映画を指す。

17 **lift**「高揚させる」

18 **Jazz Age**「ジャズ・エイジ」第一次世界大戦後から大恐慌までの、ジャズが流行し、自由で退廃的な雰囲気に満ちた時代。

created was surely *Top Hat* (1935). All its sets were beautifully designed in pure Art Deco, which represented *modernity* and a *belief in social and technological progress*. Additionally, *Top Hat* starred the legendary dance team of Fred Astaire and Ginger Rogers, and its music was provided by the most prolific composer of "jazz standards" in history, Irving Berlin. 25

The song and dance number with the most pleasing and healthy social significance was undoubtedly Berlin's "Isn't This a Lovely Day?". In it, the two protagonists, Dale (Rogers) and Jerry (Astaire) have taken refuge in an Art Deco gazebo in a London park during a thunderstorm. She has been trying to avoid him, and he has been pursuing her. Jerry thinks the weather is "lovely" because the 30 heavy rain has forced them to remain together in the shelter of the gazebo. As the exquisitely choreographed dance proceeds, it comes to illustrate the attractiveness of a new, more balanced relationship between men and women: a *modern* relationship of *respect and equality between the sexes*. The spirit of equality is expressed first when Dale surprises Jerry with an unexpected strength and confidence, even 35 taking the lead at times in the dance. This spirit is also expressed by the relative "masculinity" of her clothes and their friendly handshake at the end.

36

The lyrics of the song "Isn't This a Lovely Day?" are perfectly rhymed. Noting, for example, the sudden change from sunny to stormy, Jerry sings, "The turn in the weather / will keep us together / so I can honestly say / that as far as I'm 40 concerned / it's a lovely day / and everything's okay." The full lyrics contain many useful examples for Japanese learners of English, but especially significant among them is surely the above phrase "The turn [=change] in the weather." A somewhat

---

NOTES

21 ***Top Hat*** 『トップ・ハット』マーク・サンドリッチ監督によるミュージカル映画。top hat とは、日本ではシルクハットと呼ばれる山高帽のこと。

22 **Art Deco** 「アール・デコ」1920~30 年代に欧米で流行した装飾様式。華やかな幾何学模様が特徴。

23 **Fred Astaire** 「フレッド・アステア」(1899–1987) 米国のダンサー・俳優。ブロードウェイでダンサーとして名声を確立し映画界に進出。1949 年にアカデミー特別賞を受賞。

24 **Ginger Rogers** 「ジンジャー・ロジャーズ」(1911–95) 米国のダンサー・俳優。『恋愛手帖』(1940) でアカデミー主演女優賞を受賞。

25 **Irving Berlin** 「アーヴィング・バーリン」(1888–1989) ロシア生まれの米国の作詞・作曲家。"White Christmas" や "God Bless America" などアメリカを代表する名曲を数多く作った。

28 **protagonist** 「主役、主人公」

29 **gazebo** 「東屋、見晴らし台」

32 **exquisitely** 「精妙に、洗練されて」

32 **choreographed** 「振り付けされた」

literal translation of this into Japanese might be something like "*tenki no henka*" (天気の変化). Conversely, an average Japanese learner, if asked to translate *"tenki* 45 *no henka*" into English would probably use "of," rather than "in," as in "(the) change of (the) weather." In fact, however, in sentences in English in which something "changes," "in" is most often *by far* the more natural preposition to use.

To better understand the functioning of these prepositions, let us consider the difference in meaning between ①"She noticed the <u>change in the design</u>" and 50 ②"She noticed the <u>change of the design</u>." While both of the underlined expressions might reasonably be rendered in Japanese as "*dezain no henkō*" (デザインの変更), sentence ① suggests that a previous design had simply been altered in some way, while sentence ② suggests that a previous design had been deliberately replaced with an entirely new one. That is to say, a change in something suggests some 55 variation within that thing, while a change of something often suggests some sort of conscious substitution. In the case of the weather on one afternoon, changes are more likely to be felt to have been *in* it rather than *of* it.

NOTES

45 **conversely**「逆に、逆に言えば」
48 **preposition**「前置詞」
56 **variation**「変化、変異」
57 **substitution**「代用、交換」

Exercises

*F*ill *I*n the *B*lanks

日本語のヒントを参考にして（　　　　）内に最も適している前置詞を入れよう。

1. The change (　　　　　　) her company's policy, though it was quite minor, shocked her so much that she began thinking about finding a new job. （会社の方針の変更）

2. John was shocked to notice a change (　　　　　　　) her daughter's behavior after five years' absence. （娘の行動の変化）

3. After moving to Yokohama, she was kind enough to notify me of her change (　　　　　) address. （住所の変更）

4. Yesterday I lost the key (　　　　　　) my apartment and stayed overnight at a karaoke box in Kichijoji. （アパートの鍵）

5. The visitors from abroad were delighted to see cherry blossoms (　　　　　) full bloom. （満開の桜）

*T*ranslate into *J*apanese

下線部の単語に注意して、以下の文を和訳してみよう。

1. In 1906, a London newspaper reporter coined the term "suffragette" to refer to any female activist in the <u>current</u> "Votes for Women" movement.

   ....
   ....
   ....

2. Since all the data was <u>now</u> in digital format, however, the next step was automation.

   ....
   ....

3. The novel, published in 1939, was dismissed as pulp fiction by <u>contemporary</u> literary critics, but today it is generally considered to be a masterpiece.

   ....
   ....
   ....

71

Translate into English

以下の文を英訳してみよう。

1. 私は、帝都大学経済学部 (the School of Economics) の 2 年生です。

   ....
   ....
   ....

2. 昨日、村上春樹の小説を読んでレポートを書く課題が出た。村上龍のほうがよかったが、しょうがないので、『ノルウェイの森』でも読んで書こうと思う。

   ....
   ....
   ....

3. Apple のスマートフォンの機能の変化についていけなくなっている自分に、最近気づいている。

   ....
   ....
   ....

Lesson **13** 代名詞の所有格、そして冠詞の意味

Find My Tokyo (Part 1)

洗練されて優れたデザインに彩られた日本の広告。しかし、そこに記された様々な「英語」は、日本を訪れる英語のネイティヴ・スピーカーにとって奇妙に感じられることが多い。my が使われた広告コピーの英語表現を通して、代名詞の所有格、そして、冠詞の意味を考えてみよう。

Grammatical Points

- 代名詞の所有格 my, his などの用法、それと関連する冠詞 the の用法
- 英語の命令法が伝える意味

Vocabulary Check

以下の単語の定義を下から選び、その番号を〔　　〕に入れよう。

executive 〔　　〕	function 〔　　〕	mystifying 〔　　〕
reveal 〔　　〕	spacious 〔　　〕	startling 〔　　〕

1. having a large amount of space
2. very surprising, unusual, or remarkable
3. someone in a high position in a company or organization who makes decisions and puts them into action
4. very strange or mysterious, impossible to explain
5. to work or operate in a particular way
6. to make previously unknown things known to others

Find My Tokyo (Part 1)

Advertisements in Japan, in addition to the ordinary Japanese-language writing that forms the bulk of their copy, often prominently feature a single phrase in "English." It should not be surprising if visitors from English-speaking countries sometimes find this phenomenon mystifying, for that "English" is commonly so bizarre as to seem to destroy any potential effectiveness of the advertising itself. One typically startling example of this was provided by the Tokyo Metro in its 《Find my Tokyo.》 campaign.

The sentence 《Find my Tokyo.》 is startling, first of all, in its use of the *imperative mood*; the sentence is an *order*, a *command*. It appears to be saying something like "I once had my own Tokyo, but I have misplaced it somewhere, and *you* must find it! I *command* you to find it." In other words, it is basically the same phrasing as would be used by a company executive who, realizing that she has misplaced her iPhone somewhere in her very spacious office and is unable to locate it herself, shouts at her secretary "Find my iPhone!" In the case of 《Find my Tokyo.》, however, it is unclear just *who* the "I" of the "my" is supposed to be.

Actually, the use of the possessive pronoun "my" quite often seems to present a problem to Japanese learners of English. Here is a sentence, written by a Japanese university student, that once made a deep impression on me: "Yesterday, I went to Shibuya to buy my blouse." The natural question (at least for someone having very little knowledge of the Japanese language) would be: "If it was your blouse, why did you have to buy it?" What the student meant to say, of course, was "I went to Shibuya to buy a blouse for myself," but the original phrasing reveals a basic misunderstanding of the use of the possessive case.

NOTES

2 **the bulk of ~**「～の大部分」
2 **prominently**「際立って、めだって」
2 **feature**「呼び物にする、売りにする」
5 **bizarre**「奇妙な、とっぴな」
9 **imperative mood**「命令法」
11 **command**「命令する」ここでは動詞として使われている。
14 **locate**「探し出す、場所を突き止める」
16 **possessive pronoun**「所有代名詞」
23 **possessive case**「所有格」

One of the most important things to understand about the use of pronouns in the possessive case is that they function in a way quite similar to the way that the definite article "the" functions. Consider, for example, the following opening sentences of an essay written in perfect English: "One summer, I went to the zoo in Portland. Its gorilla area was interesting, but there was only one male gorilla. His head was huge." In this case, we know from the expression "the zoo in Portland" that Portland has only one zoo. Otherwise, the author would have written "a zoo in Portland." In the same way, the expression "Its gorilla area" tells us that the zoo has only one gorilla area. Otherwise, the author would have written ① "One of its gorilla areas was interesting," ② "Its gorilla areas were interesting" (i.e., all of its multiple gorilla areas were interesting), or ③ "Some of its gorilla areas were interesting." That is, the "its" in "its gorilla area" is functioning in the same way as the "the" in "the zoo in Portland," saying that there exists only one of some particular thing.

In this regard, let us next consider the "His" in "His head was huge." "His head" refers to "The (one and only) head of the (one and only) male gorilla in the (one and only) gorilla area in the (one and only) zoo in Portland." It is saying that the zoo's one and only male gorilla has only one head, which might naturally be assumed for *any* gorilla. But what if the male gorilla in that zoo happened to be famous for being bicephalic (i.e., for having two heads)? Depending on the actual size of each of the heads, the sentence would either have to be "His heads were huge" or "One of his heads was huge."

Misunderstanding of this function of possessive pronouns appears in typical student essays that begin, for example, with something like "During the summer vacation, I went to Fukuoka, and I met my relative." Here the natural question would be: "Do you actually have only one relative in the whole world?" That is, as an opening sentence, the use of "my" with the singular "relative" actually means that the writer happens to have only one relative in the whole world. Otherwise, the phrase would have to be either "one of my relatives" (if only one relative happened to have been met at that time in Fukuoka) or "some of my relatives" (if multiple relatives happened to have been met).

NOTES

26 **definite article**「定冠詞」
41 **be assumed for ~**「～であると当然想定される」
43 **bicephalic**「双頭の」

Exercises

*F*ill in the *B*lanks

（　　　）内に、a, the, his のいずれかを入れてそれぞれの英文を完成させよう。

1. Human beings are (　　　) only animals that can make use of fire.

2. I have never met (　　　) person with as great a personality as he has.

3. After Louis came back from the restroom on the bullet train, he found some of
   (　　　) belongings missing.

4. The former Secretary of State died yesterday. Keeping the party united was
   one of (　　　) most important achievements.

5. Unlike in Japan, it may at times be quite difficult to find (　　　) public
   restroom in certain other East Asian countries.

Translate into Japanese

次の英文を和訳してみよう。

1. The Board of Directors is worried about our new company policy. Create an agenda for tomorrow's meeting and email it to me by noon tomorrow.

   ....
   ....
   ....

2. During my interview with Angelina Jolie, I asked her about the new film in which she has a starring role. She said, "I do not have *a* starring role—I have *the* starring role. I am not *a* star of the movie—I am *the* star of the movie!".

   ....
   ....
   ....
   ....
   ....

3. Even though you are all still only elementary school children, you may already have some ideas about what you want to do in the future. Here is an assignment for each of you: try writing a letter to a person that you imagine might be your future adult self.

   ....
   ....
   ....
   ....
   ....
   ....

Translate into English

以下の文を英訳してみよう。

1. 去年の夏、スペインを旅行中、私は久しぶりに旧友に出くわした。

   ....

   ....

   ....

2. 「じゃあ、今度の土曜日、駅中の本屋の前で会おう」
   「どちらの？　二つあるんだけれど」

   ....

   ....

   ....

3. 一族の中で、幸一だけが大学に進学した。東京の大学に出発する前に彼が受け取った親
   戚からのお祝いは、軽く 20 万円を超えた。

   ....

   ....

   ....

Lesson 14

my の用法を通して英語の感覚にせまる

Find My Tokyo (Part 2)

マイカー、マイブームなど、英語から派生し日本語の語彙になった表現は、日本人が話し、書く英語に影響を与えている。そのせいか、日本語で「マイ」を使う状況を英語で表現するとき、my を用いてしまい、結果として存在しない英文ができあがってしまうことが実に多い。前章に引き続き、my の用法を通して、英語の感覚にせまってみよう。

Grammatical Points

- 代名詞の所有格 my の用法
- my から派生した「マイ」を使った和製英語の問題

Vocabulary Check

以下の単語の定義を下から選び、その番号を [　　] に入れよう。

concise [　　]	immediate [　　]	originally [　　]
plural [　　]	significant [　　]	specifically [　　]

1. from or in the beginning

2. happening or done without delay

3. denoting more than one

4. short and clear

5. in a concrete way with respect to particular details

6. having an important effect or meaning

Find My Tokyo (Part 2)

40

In the previous lesson, we considered the use of "my" in the following opening sentence of a typical student essay: "During the summer vacation, I went to Fukuoka, and I met my relative." Because the student used "my" here with the noun "relative" in its *singular* form, the sentence suggested that this student had only one relative in the entire world. But what would the effect have been if "my" 5 had been used in reference to "relatives" in the *plural*, as in "During the summer vacation, I went to Fukuoka, and I met my relatives"? It would simply have meant that all of this student's living relatives, worldwide, had happened to be in Fukuoka at that time, and that he or she had met all of them then. The student probably should have written "met some of my relatives," "met some relatives," 10 or just "met relatives."

The most common misuse of a possessive pronoun that I find in student writing is in opening sentences like this one: "Last week, I traveled to Kyoto with *my* friend." As we have seen before, this would *actually* mean "I have only one friend in the world, and, last week, I traveled to Kyoto with that one and only friend." 15 The intended meaning in such a sentence would probably have been "I traveled to Kyoto with *a* friend [= *one of my* friends]." In the plural, it would be natural to write "with friends [= *some of my* friends / *some* friends]."

41

In conversation, problems like this involving the use of pronouns in the possessive case are usually relatively easy to overcome. In the case of a *conver-* 20 *sation* in which a speaker suddenly said, "During the summer vacation, I went to Fukuoka, and I met my relatives," a listener would assume that the speaker obviously could not actually have *meant* to say, "… I went to Fukuoka, and I met all of the relatives that I have in the entire world." That listener could then simply ask for an explanation of what had just been said, and the explanation might be 25 something like "I have an aunt and uncle who live in Fukuoka, and I met them."

With *writing*, however, a reader may be unlikely to have access to such an immediate explanation. When a learner of English is writing in the language, paying attention to the actual meaning expressed by pronouns in the possessive

NOTES ―――――――――――――――

1 **previous**「前の」
27 **access**「入手する手段・方法」

80

case can help in two ways: it can result in a clearer expression of intended 30
meaning, and it can also work to create a much more positive impression on the
reader.

This would also have been possible for the Tokyo Metro's 《Find my Tokyo.》
campaign that we considered in the previous lesson. The advertisement could
have said, in English, what it seemed to be saying in its Japanese-language copy: 35
"Discover new things for yourself to enjoy in Tokyo." Here, the *imperative mood*
would not be a problem because the use of "for yourself" softens the phrase into
more of an *encouragement to action* than a *command*.

42

With respect to many Japanese people's use of "my," however, there is a special
complicating factor to consider: the common usage in the Japanese language of 40
mai (マイ) to refer not necessarily to one's own possession of something but rather
to any individual's possession of something, as in expressions like *maihōmu* (マイ
ホーム), *maikā* (マイカー), *maibūmu* (マイブーム), and *mainanbā* (マイナンバー).

Originally, such expressions seem to have been used to give a slight emphasis
to the fact that such personal possession was a kind of "special achievement" 45
(*maihōmu*, *maikā*). This has since been extended to an emphasizing of the "personal
individuality" of the possession, as in *maibūmu*. Finally, we can see something
very different in the creation of the term *mainanbā*. Here, the thinking appears to
have been that such use of *wasei eigo* (和製英語) would have a "softening" effect.
More specifically, knowing that there might be significant popular resistance to 50
the government's creation of a personal identity number for each citizen, some
officials appear to have thought that the term *mainanbā* would have a much less
sinister, less threatening feeling than would the term *kojinbangō* (個人番号).

In this regard, it is important to remember, however, that the target of the Tokyo
Metro's 《Find my Tokyo.》 campaign was not visitors from English speaking 55
countries—it was the general Japanese public, whose common misunderstanding
of the functions of possessive pronouns in English would make the wonderfully
concise 《Find my Tokyo.》 absolutely perfect.

NOTES

37 **soften** 「和らげる」
50 **resistance** 「抵抗感、反対」
53 **sinister** 「不吉な、悪意のある」
53 **threatening** 「脅すような、威嚇的な」

Exercises

*F*ill in the *B*lanks

日本語を参考に（　　　　）内に適切な語句を入れてそれぞれの英文を完成させよう。

1. 東京でマイホームを持つのは、年々難しくなっている。

   It has been getting more difficult year by year to own (　　　　　　　　　　　).

2. 10年の貯金生活の後、私はついにマイカーを購入した。

   After a decade of saving, I finally bought (　　　　　　　).

3. 私の姉はマイカー通勤している。

   My sister goes to work (　　　　　　　　).

4. マイナンバーカードを紛失した場合、コールセンターに連絡し、一時利用停止を頼むべきである。

   If you lose your (　　　　　　　　　　　　) Card, you should contact the Call Center and request a temporary suspension of use.

5. エリックは仕事をマイペースでするが、いつも良い業績を挙げる。

   Even though Eric works (　　　　　　　　　　　), he always produces good results.

Translate into Japanese

次の名言を和訳してみよう。

1. It is lovely, when I forget all birthdays, including my own, to find that somebody remembers me. (Ellen Glasgow)

   ....
   ....
   ....

2. Patriotism is when love of your own people comes first; nationalism, when hate for people other than your own comes first. (Charles de Gaulle)

   ....
   ....
   ....

3. I don't know if there is a personal identity. We all imagine that we are absolute individuals. But when we begin to look for where this individuality resides, it's very difficult to find. (John Banville)

   ....
   ....
   ....
   ....

Translate into English

以下の文を英訳してみよう。

1. 行きつけの医者に代わって、東都大学病院の名医が私の手術を担当した。

....
....
....

2. 私の最近のマイブームは、60年代ロックのレコードの収集だ。レコードプレーヤーは持っていないんだけれど。

....
....
....

3. 和製英語は、英語圏ではほとんどすべて理解されないと考えたほうがいい。

....
....
....

Lesson 15 「愛と性」の英語

Love and Sexuality

> フェミニズム、LGBTQ など、社会運動の先駆けとなった「サマー・オブ・ラブ」。ビートルズが活躍した 1960 年代に起こったこの文化的・政治的な現象は、ヴェトナム反戦運動などにも波及していき、世界を動かした。若者が主導権をとり、愛と性の革命を目指した時代を垣間見ながら、「愛と性」に関する英語表現について考えてみよう。

Grammatical Points

- 愛と性に関する英語表現が持つ微妙なニュアンス
- 恋愛や結婚に関連する英語の語彙

Vocabulary Check

以下の単語の定義を下から選び、その番号を［　　］に入れよう。

deliberately ［　　］	exhilaration ［　　］	phenomenon ［　　］
prosecution ［　　］	segment ［　　］	simplistic ［　　］

1. intentionally, not by chance
2. treating complex issues as if they were much simpler than they actually are
3. a single item within the broadcast of a television or radio program
4. a person or thing that is impressive or unusual
5. a feeling of joyful excitement
6. the continuation of a course of action with a view to its completion, often that of a war

85

Love and Sexuality

43

In June of 1967, NHK participated in an event that was groundbreaking in the history of media. It joined the national broadcasters of 13 other countries, from Austria to Australia, in producing and airing the world's first live, multinational, multi-satellite television program. The show was called *Our World* and was viewed by hundreds of millions of people across the globe. Today it is most ₅ famous (as it soon became even then) for a single program segment, the Beatles performance of the song "All You Need Is Love," which was composed by John Lennon for use in the show.

The lyrics of "All You Need Is Love" are both simple and simplistic, and they were made so deliberately, in consideration of what was expected to be the ₁₀ program's extensive non-English-speaking audience. The "Love" of the title does not refer to romantic or sexual love; rather, it suggests a kind of utopian ideal of a feeling of humanity and compassion towards one's fellow human beings.

The broadcast of *Our World* coincided with the worldwide social phenomenon known as the "Summer of Love." In reference to this phenomenon, the *San* ₁₅ *Francisco Oracle* newspaper wrote at the time, "A new concept of celebrations beneath the human underground must emerge, become conscious, and be shared, so a revolution can be formed with a renaissance of compassion, awareness, and love, and the revelation of unity for all mankind." These are noble ideals, but the "Summer of Love" also stood for something far more physical, the "free love" ₂₀

NOTES

1 **groundbreaking**「画期的な、草分けの」
3 **air**「放送［放映］する」
7 **compose**「作曲する、創作する」
7 **John Lennon**「ジョン・レノン」(1940–80) 英リヴァプール生まれ。ポール・マッカートニーらとロックバンド、ザ・ビートルズを結成し、1962 年にレコード・デビュー。世界中で爆発的な人気を呼び、社会現象を引き起こす。70 年の解散後、レノンは日本人の妻オノ・ヨーコと活動を行うが、1980 年 12 月 8 日、自宅前でファンを名乗る男に撃たれ死去。
11 **extensive**「膨大な」
14 **coincide with ~**「~と同時期に起こる」
18 **renaissance**「復興、再生、復活」
18 **compassion**「同情、あわれみ」
19 **revelation**「新たな発見、啓示」
20 **physical**「身体的な、肉体的な」

movement, which was meant to liberate humanity from many of its traditional restrictions on sexual activity. The "sexual revolution" of the 1960s became closely tied to various feminist causes and eventually also led to far greater rights for members of the LGBTQ community.

There is another important kind of love that is neither utopian nor sexual: romantic love. Two years before the "Summer of Love," a classic American film set during the Civil War was released. It was entitled *Shenandoah* and was very clear in its humanitarian and antiwar attitudes, for which it came to be increasingly admired, particularly as opposition to American prosecution of the Vietnam War continued to grow.

It also had a point to make about romantic love, however, as is illustrated in one of its most famous scenes, one in which a father (Charlie) has a conversation with his daughter's suitor (Sam):

Sam: I want to ask for your daughter's hand in marriage.
Charlie: Why? Why do you want to marry her?
Sam: Well, I love her.
Charlie: That's not good enough. Do you like her?
Sam: I just said I ….
Charlie: No, no. You said you loved her. There is some difference between love and like. You see, Sam, when you love a woman without liking her, the night can be long and cold, and contempt comes up with the sun.

Truly liking a person, as a person, is, to be sure, far more likely to be long-lasting than the feeling commonly known as romantic love. For one thing, it is far easier to forgive the slightly irritating eccentricities and small faults of a good friend than it is to forgive those found in someone who has been seen as a kind of

NOTES

21 **liberate**「自由にする、開放する」
22 **restriction**「制限、拘束」
27 *Shenandoah*「邦題：『シェナンドー河』」1965 年に公開された米映画。南北戦争期のヴァージニア州を舞台にした西部劇映画。アンドリュー・V・マクラグレン監督、ジェームズ・スチュアート主演。
31 **as is illustrated in ~**「~で示されているように」
33 **suitor**「求婚者」
34 **ask for ~'s hand (in marriage)**「~に結婚を申し込む」
41 **contempt**「軽蔑、侮蔑」

romantic ideal.

45

On the other hand, romantic love, especially "new love," is certainly likely to be far more exciting than a friendship. And its exhilaration can bring on feelings like those expressed in Roberta Flack's timeless hit song of 1974, "Feel Like Makin' Love": "Strolling in the park, watching winter turn to spring / walking in 50 the dark, seeing lovers do their thing, / that's the time I feel like making love to you." In modern English, the expression "making love to (someone)" is explicitly sexual. Basically, it simply refers to the act of sexual intercourse.

For Japanese students of the English language, there is, in this regard, one vocabulary item that may deserve a little more care than it is sometimes given: 55 *koibito* (恋人). In Japanese, a young person might refer to a boyfriend or girlfriend with whom she/he has a romantic relationship as a *koibito*, but, in English, referring to that boyfriend or girlfriend as "my lover" would be fundamentally equivalent to saying "my sexual partner." Though one's relationship with a *koibito* may indeed be sexual, the term *koibito*, unlike "lover," is not necessarily used to 60 stress sexuality. Generally speaking, "boyfriend" and "girlfriend" will always be safer vocabulary choices, even for older adults.

NOTES ——————————

49 **Roberta Flack**「ロバータ・フラック」(1937–) 米ノース・カロライナ州出身のソウル・シンガー。"The First Time Ever I Saw Your Face"（「愛は面影の中に」）、"Killing Me Softly with His Song"（「やさしく歌って」）などのヒット曲がある。

50 **stroll**「ぶらつく、散歩する」

52 **explicitly**「あからさまに」

58 **fundamentally**「根本的に」

59 **equivalent**「同等の」

Exercises

Fill in the Blanks

日本語を参考に、下の {   } から適切な語句を選んで（   ）内に入れてみよう。

1. 父親とヴァージン・ロードを歩いているとき、イレーンは、この上なく幸せだった。

Elaine couldn't have been happier when she walked down (   ) with her father.

2. 我々は、それまで誰も歩いたことのない歩道を歩いた。

   We walked down what until then had been (   ).

3. ボブは、テイラー・スウィフトのコンサートに行く相手を見つけることができなかった。

   Bob couldn't find a (   ) to go with to the Taylor Swift concert.

4. 彼女は、父親と同じ年の愛人とレストランにいるところを母親に目撃された。

   She was spotted by her mother in a restaurant with a (   ) the same age
   as her father.

5. 昔気質の私の祖父は、ポールの配偶者がスコットランド出身の男性だと聞いて驚いた。

   My old-fashioned grandfather was surprised when he heard Paul's (   )
   was a man from Scotland.

{ lover,   spouse,   a "virgin" footpath,   date,   the aisle }

Translate into Japanese

次の名言を和訳してみよう。

1. It is better to be hated for what you are than to be loved for what you are not.

   (Andre Gide)

   ....
   ....

2. A successful marriage requires falling in love many times, always with the
   same person. (Mignon McLaughlin)

   ....
   ....

3. "I'm not sentimental—I'm as romantic as you are. The idea, you know, is that the sentimental person thinks things will last—the romantic person has a desperate confidence that they won't." (F. Scott Fitzgerald)

....
....
....
....

Translate into English

以下の文を英訳してみよう。

1. 世論調査によると、経済的な事情から結婚をしない人が増えているという。

....
....

2. 古代ギリシャの時代から、哲学者たちは、恋愛について真剣に論じてきた。

....
....

3. 日本のテレビ番組、漫画、アニメは、欧米に比べて性描写に対して寛容だと言われてきたが、これも変わりつつある。

....
....
....

English Lessons with Mark Petersen

マーク・ピーターセンの英語レッスン

編著者　　　マーク・ピーターセン

発行者　　　山　口　隆　史

発 行 所　　　株式会社 音羽書房鶴見書店

〒113-0033　東京都文京区本郷 3-26-13
TEL 03-3814-0491
FAX 03-3814-9250
URL: https://www.otowatsurumi.com
e-mail: info@otowatsurumi.com

2023 年 3 月 1 日　　初版発行
2023 年 4 月 1 日　　2 刷発行

組版　ほんのしろ
装幀　大谷治之 (オセロ)
印刷・製本　(株)シナノ

■ 落丁・乱丁本はお取り替えいたします。　　　E-148